WELFARE

OPPOSING
VIEWPOINTS®

Other Books of Related Interest

Opposing Viewpoints Series

Abortion
Adoption
An Aging Population
AIDS
American Government
American Values
America's Children
America's Cities
America's Future
America's Victims
Child Abuse
Civil Liberties
Drug Abuse
Economics in America
Education in America

The Family in America
Feminism
Health Care in America
The Homeless
Illegal Immigration
Interracial America
The Legal System
Male/Female Roles
Politics in America
Population
Poverty
Race Relations
Social Justice
Violence
Work

Current Controversies Series

Family Violence
Genetics and Intelligence
Hunger
Illegal Immigration
Youth Violence

At Issue Series

Affirmative Action
Domestic Violence
Immigration Policy
Single-Parent Families
Voting Behavior
Welfare Reform

WELFARE

OPPOSING VIEWPOINTS®

David Bender & Bruno Leone, *Series Editors*

Charles P. Cozic, *Book Editor*
Paul A. Winters, *Book Editor*

OPPOSING
VIEWPOINTS®
SERIES

Greenhaven Press, Inc., San Diego, CA

Photo credit: Craig McClain

Greenhaven Press, Inc.
PO Box 289009
San Diego, CA 92198-9009

Library of Congress Cataloging-in-Publication Data

Welfare : opposing viewpoints / Charles P. Cozic, Paul A.
  Winters, book editors.
      p.   cm. — (Opposing viewpoints series)
  Includes bibliographical references and index.
  ISBN 1-56510-519-2 (pbk. : alk. paper). —
  ISBN 1-56510-520-6 (lib. bdg. : alk. paper)
    1. Public Welfare—United States—Philosophy. 2. Public
Welfare—Law and legislation—United States. 3. United
States—Social policy. 4. United States—Economic policy.
I. Cozic, Charles P., 1957-   . II. Winters, Paul A., 1965-   .
III. Series: Opposing viewpoints series (Unnumbered)
HV95.W453   1997
362.5'8'0973—dc20
                                                              96-31261
                                                              CIP

"Congress shall make no law . . .
abridging the freedom of speech,
or of the press."

First Amendment to the U.S. Constitution

The basic foundation of our democracy is the First Amendment
guarantee of freedom of expression. The Opposing Viewpoints
Series is dedicated to the concept of this basic freedom and the
idea that it is more important to practice it than to enshrine it.

Contents

Page

Why Consider Opposing Viewpoints?   9

Introduction   12

Chapter 1: Is Welfare Necessary?
Chapter Preface   16
1. Welfare Should Be Preserved   17
   Clarissa Pinkola Estés
2. Welfare Should Be Reformed   22
   Bill Clinton
3. Welfare Should Be Expanded   29
   Jane Haddam
4. Welfare Should Be Eliminated   35
   Michael Tanner
5. Single Mothers Need Adequate Welfare   42
   Valerie Polakow
6. Single Mothers Do Not Need Welfare   49
   George Liebmann
7. Charitable Aid Should Replace
   Government Welfare   56
   Marvin Olasky
8. Charitable Aid Cannot Replace
   Government Welfare   65
   Fred Kammer
Periodical Bibliography   72

Chapter 2: Does Welfare Encourage Dependency?
Chapter Preface   74
1. The High Value of Welfare Benefits Keeps
   the Poor on Welfare   75
   Michael Tanner, Stephen Moore & David Hartman
2. A Lack of Opportunities Keeps the Poor
   on Welfare   83
   Chris Tilly & Randy Albelda
3. Government Programs Help Teen Mothers
   Get Off Welfare   89
   Pat Rowe
4. Government Programs Do Not Help Teen
   Mothers Get Off Welfare   96
   Douglas J. Besharov & Karen N. Gardiner
Periodical Bibliography   103

Chapter 3: Is Abuse of the Welfare System a Serious Problem?

Chapter Preface   105

1. Welfare Is a Way of Life for Some Women   106
   Rachel Wildavsky & Daniel R. Levine

2. Welfare Is a Necessity for Some Women   114
   Rita Henley Jensen

3. Noncustodial Fathers Should Be Required to Support Their Children   122
   Paul Offner

4. Most Noncustodial Fathers Support Their Children   126
   Jenifer Rachel

5. Immigrants Should Be Denied Welfare   132
   Robert Rector & William F. Lauber

6. Immigrants Are Not a Heavy Burden on the Welfare System   136
   Julian L. Simon

7. Corporate Welfare Should Be Abolished   140
   Stephen Moore & Dean Stansel

8. Corporate Subsidies Are Beneficial   146
   Rob Norton

Periodical Bibliography   150

Chapter 4: How Should the Welfare System Be Reformed?

Chapter Preface   152

1. Welfare Reform Should Discourage Illegitimate Births   153
   Douglas J. Besharov

2. Welfare Reform Should Not Punish Women for Having Children   157
   Mimi Abramovitz

3. Welfare Recipients Should Be Trained and Required to Work   164
   Judith M. Gueron

4. Job Training Programs Are Ineffective   172
   Spencer Rich

5. Welfare Should Be Turned Over to the States   178
   John Engler

6. Welfare Should Not Be Turned Over to the States   182
   Daniel Patrick Moynihan

7. Welfare Reform Should Promote Personal
   Responsibility   186
       Tommy G. Thompson

8. Welfare Reform Should Serve the Needs
   of the Poor   190
       Lynn Woolsey

Periodical Bibliography   194

For Further Discussion   195
Organizations to Contact   197
Bibliography of Books   201
Index   203

Why Consider Opposing Viewpoints?

"The only way in which a human being can make some approach to knowing the whole of a subject is by hearing what can be said about it by persons of every variety of opinion and studying all modes in which it can be looked at by every character of mind. No wise man ever acquired his wisdom in any mode but this."

John Stuart Mill

In our media-intensive culture it is not difficult to find differing opinions. Thousands of newspapers and magazines and dozens of radio and television talk shows resound with differing points of view. The difficulty lies in deciding which opinion to agree with and which "experts" seem the most credible. The more inundated we become with differing opinions and claims, the more essential it is to hone critical reading and thinking skills to evaluate these ideas. Opposing Viewpoints books address this problem directly by presenting stimulating debates that can be used to enhance and teach these skills. The varied opinions contained in each book examine many different aspects of a single issue. While examining these conveniently edited opposing views, readers can develop critical thinking skills such as the ability to compare and contrast authors' credibility, facts, argumentation styles, use of persuasive techniques, and other stylistic tools. In short, the Opposing Viewpoints Series is an ideal way to attain the higher-level thinking and reading skills so essential in a culture of diverse and contradictory opinions.

In addition to providing a tool for critical thinking, Opposing Viewpoints books challenge readers to question their own strongly held opinions and assumptions. Most people form their opinions on the basis of upbringing, peer pressure, and personal, cultural, or professional bias. By reading carefully balanced opposing views, readers must directly confront new ideas as well as the opinions of those with whom they disagree. This is not to simplistically argue that everyone who reads opposing views will—or should—change his or her opinion. Instead, the series enhances readers' depth of understanding of their own views by encouraging confrontation with opposing ideas. Careful examination of others' views can lead to the readers' understanding of the logical inconsistencies in their own opinions, perspective on why they hold an opinion, and the consideration of the possibility that their opinion requires further evaluation.

Evaluating Other Opinions

To ensure that this type of examination occurs, Opposing Viewpoints books present all types of opinions. Prominent spokespeople on different sides of each issue as well as well-known professionals from many disciplines challenge the reader. An additional goal of the series is to provide a forum for other, less known, or even unpopular viewpoints. The opinion of an ordinary person who has had to make the decision to cut off life support from a terminally ill relative, for example, may be just as valuable and provide just as much insight as a medical ethicist's professional opinion. The editors have two additional purposes in including these less known views. One, the editors encourage readers to respect others' opinions—even when not enhanced by professional credibility. It is only by reading or listening to and objectively evaluating others' ideas that one can determine whether they are worthy of consideration. Two, the inclusion of such viewpoints encourages the important critical thinking skill of objectively evaluating an author's credentials and bias. This evaluation will illuminate an author's reasons for taking a particular stance on an issue and will aid in readers' evaluation of the author's ideas.

As series editors of the Opposing Viewpoints Series, it is our hope that these books will give readers a deeper understanding of the issues debated and an appreciation of the complexity of even seemingly simple issues when good and honest people disagree. This awareness is particularly important in a democratic society such as ours in which people enter into public debate to determine the common good. Those with whom one disagrees should not be regarded as enemies but rather as people whose views deserve careful examination and may shed light on one's own.

Thomas Jefferson once said that "difference of opinion leads to inquiry, and inquiry to truth." Jefferson, a broadly educated man, argued that "if a nation expects to be ignorant and free . . . it expects what never was and never will be." As individuals and as a nation, it is imperative that we consider the opinions of others and examine them with skill and discernment. The Opposing Viewpoints Series is intended to help readers achieve this goal.

David L. Bender & Bruno Leone,
Series Editors

Introduction

"Continued dependence upon relief induces a spiritual and moral disintegration fundamentally destructive to the national fibre."

—*Franklin Delano Roosevelt*

"To look at 'welfare' recipients as the cause of the nation's ills is to be blind to larger economic trends and shifts."

—*Network*

When welfare programs were begun in the mid-1930s, President Roosevelt expressed concern that the poor would become dependent on government handouts. His solution, as described by Mickey Kaus, contributing editor of the *New Republic*, was to create the Works Progress Administration (WPA), which initiated programs that provided public jobs to the able-bodied poor and that required work in exchange for assistance. Though the WPA ended in 1943, moving recipients off the welfare rolls and into jobs has remained the goal of the welfare system. Nevertheless, as contemporary observers—liberals and conservatives alike—point out, many welfare recipients spend long periods of time collecting government aid. Social conservatives, on the one hand, contend that welfare recipients become dependent on aid because the generous benefits provide a more financially attractive way of life than work does. Liberal supporters of welfare, on the other hand, maintain that those in need are trapped in poverty because neither the system nor the low-wage work available to them enables them to overcome poverty.

Welfare's detractors have long argued that the system promotes dependency. Conservatives contend that because welfare provides the basic necessities of life without requiring work, those receiving public assistance have no reason to find jobs and become self-supporting. The only way to encourage the welfare-dependent poor to obtain jobs, these critics argue, is to end the welfare system. Bruce Fein, a conservative columnist and lawyer, asserts, "The vast majority of recipients would discover the resolve and initiative needed for employment if the alternative were stark subsistence or less."

Michael Tanner and Stephen Moore of the libertarian Cato Institute maintain that the problem is not that welfare is an attractive option for those unwilling to work but that "welfare pays better than work." They contend that the benefits paid by aid programs exceed the income that could be obtained by working and afford recipients a comfortable standard of living. According to a 1995 analysis by Tanner and Moore, a package of the six most common types of welfare assistance pays substantially more than an entry-level job—and is provided tax free. The welfare packages of some states, they estimate, exceed even the salaries of many conventional jobs, such as teaching or secretarial positions. Welfare recipients—even those willing and able to work—make more money if they stay on welfare for as long as they can, the authors assert. Like Fein, Tanner and Moore advocate reducing the level of benefits for recipients.

Counter to such arguments, welfare advocates assert that welfare does not provide anything close to a comfortable standard of living. They maintain that the most commonly used form of welfare, Aid to Families with Dependent Children (AFDC), pays less than half the amount necessary for the typical welfare family to subsist. According to Marian Wright Edelman, president of the Children's Defense Fund, "The average [AFDC] grant that a family of three receives per year . . . is far below the federal poverty level. When combined with food stamps, the maximum total benefit in a typical state is still only 70 percent of the poverty line." Edelman contends that it is necessary to raise the level of aid to the poor in order to help them overcome poverty.

Liberals also dispute the contention that welfare promotes dependency, arguing instead that economic conditions keep the poor trapped between low-wage work and temporary reliance on assistance. Edelman maintains that contrary to the stereotype of the long-term welfare dependent, 70 percent of recipients leave the rolls for a job within two years' time. She notes, however, that some do return to the system because low-wage work does not provide them with medical benefits or sufficient income. In many states, Edelman explains, welfare recipients lose aid benefits if they take even a minimum-wage job. According to Network, a liberal Catholic social justice lobbying group, a minimum-wage job does not provide the typical welfare beneficiary—a mother with two children—with the income necessary to rise out of poverty. In Network's view, "Many AFDC recipients cannot find work that does not drive them further into poverty." To help the needy rise out of poverty, defenders of welfare contend, it is necessary to create good paying jobs and to ameliorate the economic factors that cause poverty.

Though conservatives and liberals agree on the goal of moving people from welfare to productive jobs, they disagree on the measures necessary to achieve that goal. While breaking the habit of dependency is paramount for detractors of welfare, helping the needy to maintain a decent standard of living is the primary concern for welfare advocates. *Welfare: Opposing Viewpoints* presents both sides of the debate in the following chapters: Is Welfare Necessary? Does Welfare Encourage Dependency? Is Abuse of the Welfare System a Serious Problem? How Should the Welfare System Be Reformed? Contributors to these chapters present arguments on the benefits and drawbacks of the welfare system.

Is Welfare Necessary?

Chapter Preface

When Aid to Families with Dependent Children (AFDC) was created in 1935, beneficiaries numbered one-half million. In 1995, approximately 14 million Americans—two-thirds of them children—received more than $20 billion in AFDC benefits.

Critics of government welfare argue that despite $5 trillion spent on antipoverty programs since the 1960s, more Americans than ever are now dependent on welfare. Some conservatives, including former U.S. education secretary William J. Bennett, contend that because the welfare system has failed miserably, the time has come to eliminate public-assistance programs. According to Bennett, the welfare system—"the most pernicious government program of the past quarter century"—should be abolished. Instead, he maintains, private charities and family members should support the poor and encourage them to become self-sufficient.

Other Americans, however, defend government welfare as a crucial safety net for the needy. In the words of syndicated columnist Jimmy Breslin, "The welfare system has worked brilliantly. It has fed and housed the helpless. That is exactly what it was supposed to do." Breslin and other welfare advocates contend that government welfare is the ideal means to care for the poor.

But many experts argue that, although welfare should not be eliminated, it does need drastic reform to accomplish the goal of helping the poor become self-sufficient. Proposed welfare-reform programs include limiting AFDC benefits to a two-year period and making benefits contingent on parents' participation in job-training programs and their children's consistent school attendance. Advocates maintain that these programs will reduce the number of people who are in need of government assistance.

While America's poor will always depend on some form of financial assistance, experts disagree over what role, if any, government should play. The authors in this chapter examine whether the welfare system is necessary.

"*[Mercy] means to care, to care for those who need, and especially to take care in dealing with them.*"

Welfare Should Be Preserved

Clarissa Pinkola Estés

In the following viewpoint, Clarissa Pinkola Estés argues that the welfare system is a vital—and often the only—source of support for the poor. Estés recounts her experience as a divorced single mother who relied on welfare while she was working and attending college. She warns that welfare reforms that cut essential services will prevent other poor people from bettering their lives as she did. Estés, a certified Jungian psychoanalyst in Denver, Colorado, is the author of *The Gift of Story* and the best-selling *Women Who Run with the Wolves*.

As you read, consider the following questions:

1. How is society judged, according to Estés?
2. How long did Estés and her child receive food stamps?
3. With what does the author equate government "helps"?

Abridged from Clarissa Pinkola Estés, "Witness for Mercy: A Testimony to the 104th Congress," *Creation Spirituality*, Summer 1995. Reprinted with permission.

I had heard in late January 1995 that there were hearings being planned on welfare reform in Washington, and having heard so many deleterious slurs against those on welfare, felt I might be able to help in some way.

A 43-page welfare reform bill had been introduced in the House of Representatives that would, among many other sufferings, hinder school hot lunch programs, eliminate help for mothers under 18 years of age, cut pitifully small payments to severely disabled children and cause them to be institutionalized instead of being cared for at home by their parents. The bill would completely drop through the chasms of Congress's reckless rush to "cut now and question later," the working poor and the corporately dislocated, the disenfranchised factory workers and miners, and hundreds of other families who have fallen on hard times or who are untrained, uneducated, forlorn and often hope-lost. [The bill failed to become law.]

Why I Went to Washington

Additionally and perhaps most egregiously, many congressional representatives of the "new Congress" were advocating that women be "re-stigmatized" for being single mothers (once having been married) or for having given birth to children without being married to the child's father—often having been abandoned by the child's father—that "uneducated people ought to be shamed out of needing aid," that the Great Society programs (that educate the poor and train them for far more than just turning hamburgers) had failed and ought to be done away with, and—as uncivil commentators hyped it and too many congressmen took up the slur—that women with children who were on assistance were "welfare queens."

While it is very true that there is abuse of welfare and that there is far more criminal activity in and around welfare than most legislators have ever imagined, and that all of this must absolutely be pried out and straightened out, the representatives in Congress were attempting to disenfranchise children, old people, and the helpless in ways that cannot be tolerated in any true society that aspires toward greatness. We can see throughout history that society is judged by its citizens and by history alike—not by its wars won, not by its Gross National Product, but by how it treats its old people, its war veterans, its children, its immigrants, its minorities, its families, its helpless, its artists and its disenfranchised.

I contacted the offices of Rep. Patricia Schroeder (D-Colo.), who supported my "participating in the welfare reform debate as a witness . . . as a 'welfare success story'. . . whose testimony will help many of us understand this difficult, yet important issue.". . .

Following is my testimony, most of which I was able to enter into the formal *Congressional Record.*

Thank you distinguished committee members. I am a psychoanalyst who has been practicing clinically for over 20 years. However, 25 years ago, I was either—you decide—I was either what I have heard some recently call "America's worst nightmare, a welfare queen,"—and if I was a queen back then, I want a crown; I did not get one then—or else I am what I believe myself to be, and what I think hundreds of thousands of other people who went through the Great Society programs together with me are: I think that we are America's best dreams come true.

Unattractive, but Necessary

Winston Churchill once said that democracy was a flawed political system, but less flawed than any other. The same might be said of welfare in a capitalist economy. As distasteful and degrading as public assistance is, it is less distasteful and degrading than people begging, stealing and starving on the streets. To pretend otherwise is demagoguery and will surely lead to tragedy.

Peter Barnes, *Los Angeles Times,* March 13, 1995.

Now, these many, many years later, I hold a doctorate degree, and a postdoctorate diploma. But 25 years ago, I had nothing.

I am a Latina, and I come from a non-literate family; good people, wise people who could not read or write, or who did so haltingly. I was the first in my family to be able to gain a high school diploma. But even so, as a young woman I came to be in desperate circumstances, very difficult ones.

Needing Help

Twenty-five years ago, after a divorce and with a little tiny child, I needed to ask for help. Imagine a vast ocean if you would, one that had to be crossed in order for me to have a decent life for myself and my child. Many think that crossing from the underclass to the middle class is just a matter of wading across a small stream or swimming across a narrow point in a river. This is not so. Between the classes there is an enormous ocean that separates one side from the other.

So there we were at the ocean's edge, my child and I. Two souls with completely full hearts, but with an absolutely empty future.

Well, all of a sudden there came along a little raft on this ocean where there had been nothing until then, nothing except great waves and storms and dark nights. This little raft, held together with a little of this and a little of that, was provided by the federal government. It was teeming with people hanging off the sides. What a tattered but fierce lot. Was I a strong rower? I could and would row until I felt my arms would break, and then I would row some more. And so we did set off, and I did row . . . we all did row for all we were worth.

Journal Notes

I'd like to read to you briefly a few of the notes from my journal of that time:

- Food Supplements . . . once a month I go down into the most dangerous part of town. They give us a large block of processed cheese and a big box of powdered milk. It is such good protein.
- Project Child: Federal free "well baby" care for my little daughter until she is five years old, though no health care for us adults, no health insurance either. But I pray to stay healthy.
- Food stamps, I am grateful for these. I cannot take one more job. I have three already and school full-time. "Help Me Make It Through the Night" isn't just a love song.
- No child care or day care possible. $2.50 an hour might sound like a lot, but the cost of babysitters will take all three paychecks and then some. I am taking my baby to college in a little carrier on my back. I am grateful to have her. At work, people hide her for me when the boss comes.
- Two straight days and nights of excruciating pain. My jaw is still hot, swollen. Finally, I pulled two teeth I thought were the trouble. I guessed right. I can tell my fever is going way down.

Because of the six months during which my child received Aid to Families with Dependent Children and the almost two years that we were on food stamps, Project Child, Supplementary Food program, job training program, that is, work-study, and additionally receiving small $90 a quarter grants so that I could go to State college—*college*, for the first time in my life— because of these, I believe I have good insight into what it takes to assist a person who comes from the so-called "underclass," to help them so that perhaps they might cross that ocean, that enormous, dark ocean that separates the classes.

What I am asking you to do and to continue doing is to provide the little raft. I am not asking you to row. There is no outboard motor on this raft. I am not asking you to provide a yacht. Just a raft for us to go across this great gulf that separates the classes, one from the other.

You see, we cannot do it without you. We cannot do it by ourselves only. If we could, we all would have done it by now. I think that I and hundreds of thousands of other people all look for the opportunity to do everything we can do on our own behalf.

And, I might add, that when we finally do arrive on the distant shore, we will have arrived there, not through a sense of shame or through being shamed—as I have heard some people propose that the poor or the unknowing ought to be humiliated in some way—but through *pride*, through pride in ourselves as people *who could make it*, people who *could do it*. I am positive that if a person knows better, they will do better.

So, in the very end, I would say, that all these helps that are given out by the government to those who have little or nothing, these are but a boost, or a push. They are certainly not a handout, but rather most certainly, as still carries great motivation, *a hand up*.

Care and Mercy

These helps to those who have no way to rise up must continue. In business—and the government is a business—"money and management" issues are always a concern. "M&M's" as they say in the MBA programs—"M&M's," money and management. But even though it is not taught at Harvard Business School now, I am certain that it will one day, and that is that there has to be a third M in the equation of all business decisions, and that third M is for *mercy*. Mercy does not mean to give things away for free, nor to give to the undeserving. It means to care, to care for those who need, and especially to take care in dealing with them. So you decide. I am either "a welfare queen personified," in which case I definitely want a crown for I did not receive one then. Or maybe I and the hundreds of thousands of us who came through the Great Society programs, all of us who were given a chance to be educated, all the Nam vets, all the mothers with little children, all the disabled, all the poor in cash but rich in spirit, perhaps you will see that all of us are, in fact, America's best dream come true.

The Lived Truth

At the end of this speech, the gallery, which was filled with disenfranchised miners from Pennsylvania, very poor people from Appalachia, displaced factory workers from upper Michigan, black mothers and their children from D.C., broke out into a raucous applause—which was duly noted in the *Congressional Record*. The applause was not so much for me nor for my words but for the *lived truth* of those words.

"We have a chance finally to replace dependence with independence, welfare with work."

Welfare Should Be Reformed

Bill Clinton

Bill Clinton, elected the forty-second U.S. president in 1992, has long advocated reform of America's welfare system. In the following viewpoint, a speech given at a welfare reform conference in Kansas City, Missouri, on June 14, 1994, Clinton proposes to "end welfare as we know it" by requiring recipients to work, enforcing child-support measures, reducing teenage pregnancies, reforming the health care system, and strengthening families. Clinton maintains that the welfare system needs to institute such a comprehensive approach in order to prevent long-term dependence.

As you read, consider the following questions:

1. What is the total amount of uncollected child support money in America, according to Clinton?
2. In the author's opinion, what should teen parents be encouraged to do?
3. What is a popular misconception about welfare, according to Clinton?

Excerpted from Bill Clinton's speech at the Welfare Reform Conference, Kansas City, Missouri, June 14, 1994.

The challenge of the welfare system poses these issues, all of them in stark terms—how to make the economy work, how to make the government work for ordinary citizens, how to empower individuals and strengthen communities. These difficulties are all present in the challenges presented by the current welfare system. There's no greater gap between our good intentions and our misguided consequences than you see in the welfare system.

It started for the right common purpose of helping people who fall by the wayside. And believe it or not, it still works that way for some—people who just hit a rough spot in their lives and have to go on public assistance for awhile, and then they get themselves off and they do just fine. But for many the system has worked to undermine the very values that people need to put themselves and their lives back on track.

We have to repair the damaged bond between our people and their government, manifested in the way the welfare system works. We have to end welfare as we know it.

In 1994, I sent to Congress my plan to change the welfare system—to change it from a system based on dependence to a system that works toward independence—to change it so that the focus is clearly on work.

I also want to say that I developed a phrase over the last few years that would end welfare as we know it by saying welfare ought to be a second chance, not a way of life. One young woman I met a few moments ago said it ought to be a stepping stone, not a way of life. Maybe that's even better. But you have the idea.

Long before I became President, I worked with other governors and members of Congress of both parties. I worked on it with people who were on welfare, a lot of them. And let me say first of all to all those whom I invite to join this great national debate, if you really want to know what's wrong with the welfare system, talk to the people who are stuck in it or who have been on it. They want to change it more than most people you know. And if you give them half a chance, they will.

Success Stories

Before I came down to see you, I met with Yolanda Magee, and she told me her story. I also met with several other people who are now working in [Kansas City], who used to be on welfare—people who get up every morning and go to work in factories or small businesses or banks, who do their best to take care of their children and to advance their capacity to succeed in our complex, modern society. . . .

Now, every one of those American citizens at one point in her life was on welfare. Everyone now, thanks to programs and incentives and help with medical coverage and child care and training, and just helping people put their lives back together, is now a working American. And I say to you, if these American citizens can do this here in Kansas City, we ought to be able to do this in every community in the country. And we ought to be able to change the system.

Responsibility

How shall we change this system? Let me say first, I think we have to begin with responsibility—with the elemental proposition that governments do not raise children; people do. And among other things, an awful lot of people are trapped in welfare because they are raising children on their own when the other parent of the child has refused to pay child support that is due.

This plan includes the toughest child support enforcement measures in the history of this country that go after the $34 billion gap in this country. That is, it is estimated that there are $34 billion worth of ordered but uncollected child support today in America—$34 billion.

How are we going to do that? First, by requiring both parents to be identified at a hospital when a baby's born. Second, by saying, if you don't provide for your children, you should have your wages garnished, your license suspended, you should be tracked across state lines. If necessary, you should have to work off what you owe. This is a very serious thing. We can no longer say that the business of bringing a child into the world carries no responsibility with it and that someone can walk away from it.

The second thing that responsibility means is not just going after people who aren't fulfilling it, but rewarding those who are being responsible. The system now does just the opposite. Just for example—the welfare system will pay teen parents more to move out of their home than to stay there. In my opinion, that is wrong. We should encourage teen parents to live at home, stay in school, take responsibility for their own futures and their children's futures. And the financial incentives of the welfare system ought to do that instead of just the reverse. We have to change the signals we are sending here.

· Illegitimacy

We also have to face the fact that we have a big welfare problem because the rate of children born out of wedlock, where there was no marriage, is going up dramatically. The rate of illegitimacy has literally quadrupled since Daniel Patrick Moynihan, now a Senator from New York, first called it to our attention 30 years ago. At the rate we're going, unless we reverse it, within 10 years more than half of our children will be born in homes where there has never been a marriage.

24

We must keep people from the need to go on welfare in the first place by emphasizing a national campaign against teen pregnancy, to send a powerful message that it is wrong to continue this trend, that children should not be born until parents are married and fully capable of taking care of them. And this trend did not develop overnight. There are many reasons for it. It will not be turned around overnight. But be sure of this: no government edict can do it.

A New System

Welfare today has left a sad mark on the American success story. It has created a world in which children have no dreams for tomorrow and grownups have abandoned their hopes for today.

The time has come to replace this failed system with a new system that uplifts our Nation's poor, a new system that turns the social safety net from a trap into a trampoline, a new system that rewards work and personal responsibility in families, a new system that lifts a load off working, taxpaying Americans.

Bill Archer, *Congressional Digest*, June/July 1995.

This is a free country with hundreds of millions of people making their decisions, billions of them every day. To change a country on a profound issue like this requires the efforts of millions and millions and millions of you talking openly and honestly and freely about these things; talking to people who have lived through these experiences, and many of them doing the very best they can to be honorable and good parents; talking about what we can do to involve churches and civic clubs and groups of all kinds in this endeavor—not to point the finger at people to drive them down or embarrass them, but to lift them up so that they can make the most of their lives, and so they can be good parents when the time comes to do that.

But let us be clear on this: No nation has ever found a substitute for the family. And over the course of human history, several have tried. No country has ever devised any sort of program that would substitute for the consistent, loving devotion and dedication and role-modeling of caring parents. We must do this work. This is not a government mission, this is an American mission. But we must do it if we want to succeed over the long run.

Putting People to Work

And let me say finally that if you strengthen the families, we still can't change the welfare system unless it is rooted in getting people back to work. You can lecture people, you can encourage people, you can do whatever you want, but there has to be something at the end of the road for people who work hard and play by the rules. Work is the best social program this country ever devised. It gives hope and structure and meaning to our lives. All of us here who have our jobs would be lost without them.

Just stop for a moment sometime today and think about how much of your life is organized around your work—how much of your family life, how much of your social life, not to mention your work life. Think about the extent to which you are defined by the friends you have at work, by the sense that you do a good job, by the regularity of the paycheck.

One of these fine women who's agreed to come here today said that one of the best things about being off welfare was getting the check and being able to go buy her own groceries every two weeks. That's a big deal.

So I say to you, we propose to offer people on welfare a simple contract. We will help you get the skills you need, but after two years, anyone who can go to work must go to work—in the private sector, if possible; in a subsidized job, if necessary. But work is preferable to welfare. And it must be enforced.

Now, this plan will let communities do what's best for them. States can design their own programs, communities can design their own programs. This will support initiatives like the WEN [Women's Employment Network] program here, not take things away from them and substitute government programs.

We want to give communities a chance to put their people to work in child care, home care and other fields that are desperately needed. We want every community to do what you've done here in Kansas City—to bring together business and civic and church leaders together to find out how you can make lasting jobs and lasting independence.

Let me say just a couple of other things. If you wish people to go to work, you also have to reward them for doing so. Now, a popular misconception is that a lot of people stay on welfare because the welfare check is so big. In fact, when you adjust it for inflation, welfare checks are smaller than they were 20 years ago.

The Economics of Welfare

But there are things that do keep people on welfare. One is the tax burden of low wage work; another is the cost of child care; another is the cost of medical care. Now, a few years ago, I was active as a governor in helping to rewrite the welfare laws so that states were given the opportunity to offer some people the chance to get child care and medical care continued when they got off welfare and went to work for a period of transition. . . .

But we must do more. Last year [in 1993] when the Congress

passed our economic program, they expanded the earned income tax credit dramatically, which lowered taxes on one in six working Americans working for modest wages so that there would never again be an incentive to stay on welfare instead of going to work. Instead of using the tax system to hold people in poverty, we want to use the tax system to lift workers out of poverty.

That was one of the least known aspects of the economic program last year, but more than 10 times as many Missourians, for example, got an income tax cut as the 1.2 percent of the wealthiest people got an income tax increase. Why? Because you want to reward people who are out there working who are hovering just above the poverty line.

What's the next issue? In our bill, we provide some more transitional funds for child support to help people deal with that. That's important.

Health Care Reform

But thirdly, one of the most important reasons we should pass a health care reform bill that makes America join the ranks of every other advanced country in the world that provides health insurance to all its people is that today you have this bizarre situation where people on welfare, if they take a job in a place which doesn't offer health insurance, are asked to give up their children's health care, and go to work, earning money, paying taxes to pay for the health care of the children of people who didn't make the decision to go to work and stayed on welfare while they made the decision to go to work and gave up their children's health care coverage. That does not make any sense. And until we fix that, we will never close the circle and have a truly work-based system.

If we do the things we propose in this welfare reform program, even by the most conservative estimates, these changes together will move one million adults who would otherwise be on welfare into work or off welfare altogether by the year 2000.

And if we can change the whole value system, which has got us into the fix we're in today, the full savings over the long haul are more than we will ever be able to imagine, because the true issue on welfare, as Senator Moynihan said so many years ago, is not what it cost the taxpayers, it's what it cost the recipients. We should be worried about that.

And let me say, one of the most rewarding things that happened today in our little meeting before I came down was I asked all these fine ladies who are here, I said, now, if we were able to provide these services, do you believe that it should be mandatory to participate in this program? Every one of them said, absolutely. Absolutely.

Let us be honest. None of this will be easy to accomplish. We know what the problems are. And we know they did not develop overnight. But we have to make a beginning. We owe it to the next generation. We cannot permit millions and millions and millions of American children to be trapped in a cycle of dependency with people who are not responsible for bringing them into the world, with parents who are trapped in a system that doesn't develop their human capacity to live up to the fullest of their God-given abilities and to succeed as both workers and parents. We must break this cycle.

For this reason, this ought to be a bipartisan issue. Over the last 30 years, poor folks in this country have seen about all the political posturing they can stand—one way or the other. Now, there are serious people in both political parties in Congress who have advanced proposals to change the welfare system. And I really believe that we have a chance finally to replace dependence with independence, welfare with work.

An American Issue

I don't care who gets the credit for this if we can rebuild the American family; if we can strengthen our communities; if we can give every person on welfare the dignity, the pride, the direction, the strength, the sheer person power I felt coming out of these ladies that I spoke with today; if we can give people the pride that I sense from Yolanda's coworkers when she stood up here to introduce me today. This is not a partisan issue, this is an American issue.

Let me tell you, several years ago when I was a governor of my state [Arkansas], I brought in governors from all over the country to a meeting in Washington, and then I brought in people from all over America who had been on welfare to talk to them. We had most of the governors there, and they were shocked. Most of them had never met anybody who'd been on welfare before. And there was a woman from my state who was asked a question. I had no idea what she was going to answer. She was asked about her job, and she talked about her job and how she got on the job. She was asked by a governor, well, do you think enrollment in these programs ought to be mandatory? She said, I sure do.

And then a governor said, well, can you tell us what the best thing about being in a full-time job is? She said, yes, sir; when my boy goes to school, and they ask him, what does your mama do for a living, he can give an answer.

VIEWPOINT

"*The problem most middle-class Americans have with the American welfare state isn't that it supports the 'underclass.' It's that it* doesn't support anyone else."

Welfare Should
Be Expanded

Jane Haddam

In the following viewpoint, Jane Haddam argues that government-funded social services should be available to all needy people, regardless of their income. Comparing welfare in European countries and America, Haddam contends that welfare systems in Europe are superior because they offer assistance to anyone who seeks it. She maintains that middle-class Americans resent supporting the welfare system because they themselves do not receive such benefits as government-subsidized child care and medical insurance. Haddam is the author of many detective novels.

As you read, consider the following questions:

1. What hurt the position of liberal Democrats most among Connecticut voters, in Haddam's opinion?
2. To what does the author compare Western European child-care centers?
3. What change does Haddam suggest for the Head Start program?

Jane Haddam, "Promote the General Welfare," *Nation*, January 29, 1996. Reprinted with permission from the *Nation* magazine; ©1996, The Nation Company, L.P.

My husband lied to our children's pediatrician yesterday. He had to. A complicated series of events—eighteen of the worst months of both our working lives, the continued refusal of Congress to allow self-employed people to deduct any more than 25 percent of their health insurance premiums as a business expense—has left us both without insurance and persistently short of cash, mortal sins in today's health care market. Yesterday we had a very sick 2-year-old and $50 in the bank. The pediatrician costs $65 and insists on being paid at the end of each visit. My husband decided to "lose" our checkbook.

From England to Connecticut

I have been thinking a lot about health care recently. Back in 1993, when the Clinton health care plan was being debated, I was in England. My routine health care needs and those of my children were covered by the National Health Service. My children's drug prescriptions were free, and mine cost only $6.50 each. I remember reading the news from the States and feeling confident that some kind of universal health care plan would pass. Why wouldn't it? Who could possibly want to lie awake all night wondering whether she could afford to take a sick child to the doctor? Who would want to have to make a decision between buying food for the week and filling a child's $44 prescription for antibiotics?

Now that I am back in Connecticut, I realize that I have been asking the wrong questions. Most people think of Connecticut as a very rich state, but most of the money here is down on the Gold Coast, in the bedroom towns that feed New York City's corporate headquarters, or in the suburbs outside Hartford, where insurance executives live. The rest of this state, nearly three-quarters of it, is almost frighteningly marginal. The decaying industrial cities like Waterbury and Willimantic and Bristol are crammed with three-decker frame houses that get a little more dilapidated every year. The rural outposts of the northeastern corner seem to run on hope and gas stations. With the end of the cold war and the cutbacks in military spending, Connecticut has been hemorrhaging jobs the way Reagan-era S&Ls [savings and loans] hemorrhaged money. Most of the people I run into at the grocery store or the local mall either have no health insurance—because they work at jobs that don't offer benefits—or have lost over the past few years what little they did have. When grocery shopping, most of them have to decide what they can manage to do without this week: baby food or toilet paper? These are the people all my nice-girl liberal training taught me to believe would be the primary supporters of the New Deal safety net and the modern welfare state—but they aren't. Almost to a woman, they opposed the Clinton health care plan. They

30

can get positively hysterical on the subject of welfare.

Conventional wisdom lately has been that the reason middle-class American whites oppose welfare-state provisions is racism. White Americans can't stand the idea of money going to support "them." Real life is much less simple and maybe much less nasty. The welfare states of Europe support "them" too, but they have strong public support across the classes. Anyone who thinks that Western European countries are less racist than the United States ought to go live in one for a while. Germany grants citizenship on the basis of "blood" instead of residence or birth. The British Parliament looked into the suggestion of one of its members that the Crown consider paying Jamaican immigrants to go back to Jamaica. The problem most middle-class Americans have with the American welfare state isn't that it supports the "underclass." It's that it *doesn't support anyone else.*

Welfare Support in Europe

Consider what my own situation would have been over the past eighteen months if I had been a resident of any of the Western European social democracies. In the first place, those weeks when I had even less than I had this week—those weeks when I charged bread and milk on my American Express card and hoped like hell that I could pay the bill when it came in—would never have happened. France, Germany, the Netherlands and Britain all have cash-grant "child benefits" payable to anyone—rich, poor or middle class—who is raising children. This is never a huge amount of money, but it also isn't restricted (as the child tax credit would have been under Representative Richard Gephardt's plan) to parents making less than $75,000 a year. Then there is the matter of our mortgage. I have managed to pay this, on time, throughout the entire "crisis," but I have never been sure from one day to the next that I would be able to, and I never stop worrying about what would happen to us if something really awful hit—like, say, the severe illness or death of my spouse. In Britain, if I were the victim of any such catastrophe, I would go to the Social Security office and receive not only a cash grant (the dole) but whatever I needed to pay my mortgage, too. In France, I could have gone out and got a job, because I could put my children in government-sponsored day-care, which is available to all, no matter what their income.

The European welfare states are not attempts to put a safety net under the "most disadvantaged." They are by and large societywide programs available to everyone without the humiliating requirement of means tests—without, in other words, demanding that the recipient be reduced to penury and despair before receiving a minimal amount of grudgingly rendered and highly stigmatized aid. While we were in England, at least one of the Tory Members of Parliament had been on the dole within the past five years. The British dole is not a program for "them." It is a program for everybody, and that is why, in spite of the shift to the right brought about by the ascendancy of Margaret Thatcher, it has proved politically impossible to dislodge.

No Help in America

Far too many Americans know better than to go anywhere near the U.S. welfare establishment. They know that their need will not be seen as "real" need. No matter how frantically they are scrambling, they know they are not destitute enough to qualify, and they know that no matter how much they pay in taxes, no help will be available to keep them from becoming harder up than they are already. What is worse, everybody, including major spokespersons for the Democratic Party, expects them to get along without things that are deemed essential for the people who *are* destitute enough to qualify. If I were asked what had hurt the position of liberal Democrats most with the middle-class and working-class voters of Connecticut, it wouldn't be gays in the military or affirmative action or even Clinton's failed promise of a tax cut. It would be the insistence that welfare "reform" include providing welfare mothers with child care. After all, Dick Gephardt has demanded, how else can we expect welfare mothers to work? Right-minded as this might be, the women I meet in the grocery store are holding down two service jobs at the minimum wage. Their husbands (when they have them) are sometimes holding down as many as three for not much more. Nobody is providing *them* with child care.

Better to Subsidize Mothers

Mothering is work. In fact, in today's tight job market it's probably cheaper to subsidize mothers who stay home rather than pay for day care and job training for jobs that don't exist. Instead of forcing welfare moms to leave their infants for low-paying jobs, we should be pushing for expanded leave for all those who *choose* to stay home, as well as child care for workers.

Sarah Ferguson, *Village Voice*, February 1, 1994.

In fact, the list of programs for which most Americans do not qualify is endless: government-funded or subsidized health insurance, Head Start, job training, mental health services. The Clinton health care plan was supposed to provide universal medical coverage—but it wouldn't have, and most people knew it. Instead of an income-neutral system that would have applied identically and fairly to everyone, like Canada's or Germany's, it was a mess of payroll taxes, means-tested tax-relief provisions and differently priced plans that varied wildly in terms of quality and patient choice. It would have taken us from a haphazard and chaotic two-tiered system to a two-tiered system imposed by government fiat. Something similar was true of the Act for Better Child Care, shot down by conservatives during the Reagan Administration for being "socialistic." In most of Western Europe, child-care centers are like American public schools. If you want to enroll your child in one, you show up, register and satisfy the immunization requirements. The Act for Better Child Care would have constructed a paperwork nightmare of sliding-scale payments and complicated eligibility requirements, requirements that most Americans would not have been able to meet.

Provisions for All

Contrary to the inferences that might be drawn from the prevailing winds on Capitol Hill, Americans have been generally well disposed to real welfare state provisions—those that aren't means tested, so apply equally to everyone—where they have been instituted. Everybody who works contributes to the Social Security system. Everybody who contributes to the Social Security system gets a Social Security pension. The Social Security Administration does not ask its clients what other pensions they have or what other property they own in order to determine the size of Social Security checks on a sliding scale. If you want to enroll your child in your local public school, authorities will not ask you to pay tuition based on your income or refuse your child admittance because you are rich enough to afford private education.

Social Security is politically sacrosanct. The American public schools, although embattled, have not lost the loyalty of parents or students except in limited areas of the country. Problems there may be, yet nobody but the right-wing fringe wants to see either structure eliminated. Contrast that to the public's growing antagonism to "welfare," including the new surge of support for abolishing it entirely.

With the prospect of crack babies dying in garbage cans and poor mothers unable to feed their children, maybe we need to think long and hard not about protecting the "most needy" but about protecting everybody. Head Start can be expanded as a universal preschool provision, available to all children, irrespective of perceived family need. Health care can be provided under a single-payer system that treats all Americans equally. Tax credits or cash benefits for children can be provided for all Americans without finding some arbitrary income level at which to cut them off.

Real welfare states work. They have the support of their citizens by taking care to benefit their citizens—all of them. The Democratic Party, on the other hand, seems to have opted for some weird form of paternalism backed by the shrill insistence on its moral superiority to those meanspirited, heartless, selfish Republicans. Senator Tom Daschle wants to support the most needy, and if you don't, there's something wrong with you. On that basis, and that basis alone, you are supposed to vote in favor of paying higher taxes to provide the poor with medical insurance and child care that you will not be able to afford yourself. No wonder the women in my grocery store aren't Democrats. No wonder they hate government programs in general and welfare in particular. They know they are expected to fend for themselves. They know they can't afford to do that and help fund welfare, too.

In the meantime, of course, there is not only no universal health insurance plan in place but none in sight, and there isn't likely to be one as long as the Republicans are in the majority. My husband will have to go on lying to the pediatrician. I will have to go on wondering how we're ever going to be able to keep paying for those antibiotics. And all up and down my middle-class street, people will not get the medical care they need or the education that could help them better themselves or the child care that would enable them to work full-time because, in spite of all the calculations on all the pieces of paper in all the government aid offices in America that say they should be able to afford these things, real life has shown them that they can't.

=====

"We should eliminate the entire social welfare system for individuals able to work."

=====

Welfare Should Be Eliminated

Michael Tanner

The failed welfare system should not be preserved or reformed, but eliminated outright, Michael Tanner argues in the following viewpoint. Despite trillions of dollars spent on welfare since the 1960s, he contends, poverty has increased dramatically. Tanner maintains that many welfare recipients find it more advantageous to receive welfare payments than to work. The only way to break the cycle of long-term welfare dependency is to end welfare altogether, the author asserts, thereby compelling people to support themselves or seek assistance from private charities. Tanner is the director of health and welfare studies at the Cato Institute, a libertarian think tank in Washington, D.C.

As you read, consider the following questions:

1. How much has the United States spent on the poor since the War on Poverty began, according to Tanner?
2. According to Tanner, what percentage of teenage mothers go on welfare?
3. Who are the "true victims" of social welfare policies, in the author's opinion?

Excerpted from Michael Tanner, "Ending Welfare as We Know It," *Cato Policy Analysis*, July 7, 1994. Reprinted by permission of the Cato Institute.

From across the political and ideological spectrum, there is now almost universal acknowledgment that the American social welfare system has been a failure. Since the start of the War on Poverty in 1965, the United States has spent more than $3.5 trillion trying to ease the plight of the poor. What we have received for that massive investment is, primarily, more poverty.

Our welfare system is unfair to everyone: to taxpayers, who must pick up the bill for failed programs; to society, whose mediating institutions of community, church, and family are increasingly pushed aside; and most of all to the poor themselves, who are trapped in a system that destroys opportunity for them and hope for their children.

President Bill Clinton deserves credit for bringing this issue back to the forefront of the public policy debate. Yet both liberals and conservatives seem unable to understand the fundamental structural failure of welfare. Liberals continue to believe that throwing more money at current (or new) programs will make them work. Conservatives search for a paternalistic set of "incentives," such as "workfare" and "LEARNfare." Neither of those approaches is likely to solve the problems of the American social welfare system.

It is time to recognize that welfare cannot be reformed. It should be ended. There may be relatively little that can be done for people already on welfare. The key issue is to avoid bringing more people into the cycle of welfare, illegitimacy, fatherlessness, crime, more illegitimacy, and more welfare. The only way to prevent new people from entering the failed system is to abolish programs that insulate individuals from the consequences of their actions.

In 1984, Charles Murray advanced what was then a radical proposal:

> Scrapping the entire federal welfare and income-support structure for working-aged persons, including Medicaid, Food Stamps, Unemployment Insurance, Workers' Compensation, subsidized housing, disability insurance, and the rest. It would leave the working-aged person with no recourse whatsoever except the job market, family members, friends, and public or private locally funded services.

Today the case for ending welfare is stronger than ever. If President Clinton is serious about "ending welfare as we know it," he would be well advised to take Murray's thesis to heart and put an end to the failed experiment. . . .

Welfare and Poverty

What has America received in exchange for the massive antipoverty spending? Primarily, more poverty. As Figure 1 shows, the greatest strides in reducing poverty in America occurred before the advent of the social welfare state. Indeed, since 1973, poverty has actually increased, despite the continued growth in social welfare spending.

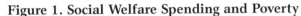

Figure 1. Social Welfare Spending and Poverty

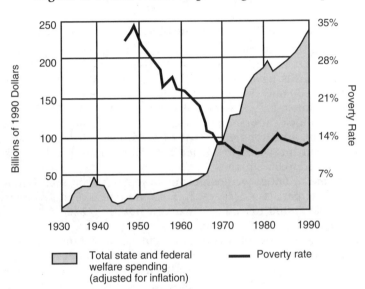

Total state and federal welfare spending (adjusted for inflation)
— Poverty rate

Source: Robert Rector, "Rethinking Welfare after the L.A. Riots," *Youth Policy*, December 1992.

There is evidence that welfare itself may prevent people from moving out of poverty. Richard Vedder and Lowell Gallaway, for example, found that only 18.3 percent of poor people receiving welfare benefits in 1987 moved out of poverty, while 45 percent of poor people who never received welfare escaped poverty.

Vedder and Gallaway suggest that while initial welfare benefits may indeed improve the standard of living for recipients—lifting them out of poverty—there eventually comes a point at which benefit levels begin to breed the types of disincentives and destructive behavior that trap recipients in poverty. That conclusion is supported by a second, more detailed study by Vedder and Gallaway of poverty and welfare benefits in six Midwestern states. That study found a 12 percent increase in the number of people living in poverty, which the authors attributed to high levels of welfare benefits.

Welfare dependence is increasingly multigenerational. Although the majority of children raised in AFDC [Aid to Families with Dependent Children] households will not receive AFDC themselves, the rate of AFDC dependence for children raised on AFDC is far higher than for their non-AFDC counterparts. For example, nearly 20 percent of daughters from families that were "highly dependent" on welfare became "highly dependent" themselves, whereas only 3 percent of daughters from non-AFDC households became "highly dependent" on welfare.

Welfare and Family

Perhaps the gravest social challenge facing America today is the skyrocketing increase in out-of-wedlock births. Out-of-wedlock births have increased by more than 400 percent since 1960. In 1960 only 5.3 percent of all births were out of wedlock. Among whites, only 2.3 percent were out of wedlock, while the out-of-wedlock rate among blacks was 23 percent. By 1990, 28 percent of all births were out of wedlock. The rate among whites had increased to 21 percent, and among blacks it had skyrocketed to 65.2 percent.

The rate of out-of-wedlock births to teenagers has nearly doubled in the past two decades. In fact, the rate of out-of-wedlock births per 1,000 unmarried women has increased faster for women aged 15 to 19 than for any other age group. . . .

Having a child out of wedlock often means a lifetime in poverty. Approximately 30 percent of all welfare recipients become such because they have an out-of-wedlock child. The trend is even more pronounced among teenage mothers. Fifty percent of all unwed teen mothers go on welfare within one year of the birth of their first child; 77 percent are on welfare within five years of the child's birth. Nearly 55 percent of AFDC, Medicaid, and food stamp expenditures are attributable to families begun by a teen birth. . . .

Spending Years on Welfare

Moreover, once on welfare, those women find it very difficult to get off. While the average length of time spent on welfare is relatively short, generally two years or less, 65 percent of persons enrolled in the program at any given time will be on the program for eight years or longer. Single mothers make up the largest portion of long-term recipients. Single women average 9.33 years on welfare and make up 39.3 percent of all recipients who are on welfare for 10 years or longer.

The noneconomic consequences of out-of-wedlock births are equally stark. There is strong evidence that the absence of a father increases the probability that a child will use drugs and engage in criminal activity. According to one study, children raised in single-parent families are one-third more likely to exhibit anti-social behavior than are children raised in two-parent families. Yet another study indicated that, holding other variables constant, black children from single-parent households are twice as likely to commit crimes as are black children from families whose fathers are present. Nearly 70 percent of juveniles in state reform institutions come from fatherless homes.

And the problem perpetuates itself. For example, white women raised in single-parent households are 164 percent more likely to bear children out of wedlock than are white women who grew up in two-parent households. Moreover, children raised in single-parent families are three times more likely than are children raised in two-parent families to become welfare recipients as adults. . . .

Welfare and Work

Contrary to stereotypes, there is no evidence that people receiving welfare are "lazy." Rather, the choice of welfare over work is often a rational decision based on the economic incentives presented. The combined tax-free value of welfare benefits is often roughly equal to the income that can be earned at many entry-level or low-paying jobs. In addition, an individual leaving welfare may suddenly forfeit medical and child-care benefits. Thus, for many, welfare may seem a perfectly reasonable alternative to work.

Studies confirm welfare as a disincentive for work. The Seattle Income Maintenance Experiment and the Denver Income Maintenance Experiment were a series of controlled experiments conducted between 1971 and 1978 to examine the effect of guaranteed income supports on the poor. Researchers concluded that every dollar of subsidy reduced labor and earnings by 80 cents. The number of hours worked declined by 43 percent for young unmarried males and 33 percent for males who later married. Unmarried women with children reduced work by 25 percent. The length of time spent outside the workforce increased by 9 weeks (27 percent) for unmarried men and by 56 weeks (60 percent) for single mothers. Other studies show that as welfare benefits increase, women are more likely to leave the labor force and enroll in welfare programs instead. . . .

Workfare Will Not Work

One program very popular among conservatives is "workfare," the requirement that welfare recipients perform public-service jobs in exchange for benefits. The belief is that such jobs will give the recipient both work experience and incentive to get off welfare. But the types of jobs envisioned under most workfare programs are unlikely to give recipients the work experience or job skills necessary to find work in the private sector. For example, New York mayor Rudolph Giuliani wants welfare recipients to perform such jobs as scrubbing graffiti and picking up trash from city streets. It is difficult to imagine graffiti scrubbers learning the skills needed to put them in demand by private employers. There seems little difference, therefore, between that type of work program and the type of government-guaranteed jobs program traditionally decried by conservatives.

Reprinted by special permission of North American Syndicate.

As for providing an incentive for recipients to get off welfare, the conservative idea is based on the stereotyped belief that welfare recipients are essentially lazy, looking for a free ride. But as seen earlier, the decision to go on welfare is more likely a result of a logical conclusion that welfare pays better than low-wage work. Since public-service jobs do little to change that earning differential, they are unlikely to convince many people to leave welfare. The Manpower Demonstration Research Corporation conducted a review of workfare programs across the country and found few, if any, employment gains among welfare participants. The general consensus of the literature on the issue, according to researchers James Heckman, Rebecca Roselius, and Jeffrey Smith, is that "mandatory work experience programs produce little long-term gain."

Another problem with workfare is that it soon runs headlong

into the desire expressed by some conservatives that women with young children stay home rather than enter the workforce. [Welfare analyst] Robert Rector, for example, opposes workfare requirements for women with children under the age of five, saying, "Great caution should be exercised toward any policy that separates young children from their mothers." But since 88.7 percent of welfare recipients are women with children under the age of five, exempting the mothers of young children eviscerates any workfare program. Rector attempts to get around that by expanding the work requirement to mothers who have been on welfare for five years or more regardless of the age of their children, but that would still not cover more than half of the recipients.

Martin Anderson, former senior economic adviser to President Ronald Reagan, sums up the simple illogic of workfare:

> If people are on welfare then, by definition, those people should be unable to care for themselves. They can't work; or the private sector can't provide jobs enough. That is supposed to be the reason they are on welfare. What sense does it make to require someone to work who cannot work?

> The idea of making people work for welfare is wrongheaded. If a person is capable of working, he should be ineligible for welfare payments. Instead of requiring men and women who are receiving fraudulent welfare payments to work, we should simply cease all payments.

. . . When it comes to charitable giving, Americans are the most generous people on earth. Every year we contribute more than $120 billion to charity. Surely, we can find private means to assist individuals who need *temporary* help.

There may be relatively little that can be done for individuals already on welfare. The key issue is to avoid bringing more people into a cycle of welfare, illegitimacy, fatherlessness, crime, and more illegitimacy. It is the children growing up in the welfare-ravaged neighborhoods who are the true victims of our social welfare policies.

We must make adoption a viable option for women who bear children they cannot afford to raise. That will entail eliminating the regulatory and bureaucratic barriers that restrict adoption today. . . .

We are not going to solve our welfare problems by throwing more money at them. Nor will it work to put welfare recipients to work in government-funded jobs picking up trash along the highways. It is time to recognize that welfare cannot be reformed. It should be ended.

Some say that would be too cruel, that it would punish the victim. But what could be crueler than sacrificing another generation to our current social welfare muddle?

"*Desperate conditions . . . are shared by millions of women and children across the country—all targets of welfare reform.*"

Single Mothers Need Adequate Welfare

Valerie Polakow

According to many welfare advocates, poor single mothers with young children are the neediest of welfare recipients. In the following viewpoint, Valerie Polakow quotes several single mothers who have struggled to live on welfare. She contends that such women—who frequently have difficulty finding jobs, obtaining child care, and continuing their education—need adequate welfare support. Polakow, author of *Lives on the Edge: Single Mothers and Their Children in the Other America*, teaches educational psychology and early childhood studies at Eastern Michigan University in Ypsilanti.

As you read, consider the following questions:

1. What is the average annual cost of child care in Michigan, according to Polakow?
2. According to the author, what is the Social Contract?
3. In Polakow's opinion, what factors force most mothers out of the labor market?

Valerie Polakow, "On a Tightrope Without a Net," *Nation*, May 1, 1995. Reprinted with permission from the *Nation* magazine; ©1995, The Nation Company, L.P.

For Deborah and her four children, homeless, all throwing up from the stomach flu at a hospital emergency room, it was the doctor's comment that was the last straw: "That just did it for me. I lost it and I just started crying when he said, 'I hope you have two bathrooms at home' and I told him, I said, 'We don't even have one bathroom—we don't even have a home—when we leave here we're going to rest under a shade tree and wait for the shelter to open for the night.' And the one nurse she recognized my pain after I started crying. I just felt so bad—I don't know, I just can't explain how I felt."

At that point Deborah's five-month odyssey of homelessness ended, and the family received emergency placement in public housing. I interviewed Deborah and other single mothers on welfare in Michigan (some of whom requested that only their first names be used) in order to document their everyday life on welfare; the multiple struggles—both material and emotional—that single mothers living and working in poverty must confront daily; the existential reality that lies behind the discourse of degradation.

Deborah describes her daily life: "It's overwhelming, I have all this pressure going on in my life. I have children in school, I'm trying to work, I'm trying to go to school, trying to do the laundry, trying to cook, trying to help the kids with their homework. Everybody is pressuring me: You know, my job wants me to work overtime; school wants this turned in, that turned in; you can't send kids to school with dirty clothes and because you live in public housing they focus on you more than normal. They stereotype your children, and if something happens, your kid gets blamed; they get treated like public-housing little animals and then, you know, the more the school treats them different the more they act different. . . . It gets to a point where you look for something to drown the pain or kill yourself, that's why some go on drugs. . . . I chose to go to community mental health."

Becoming Homeless

Yet despite Deborah's efforts to use every available community resource to cope with her destitution, and despite her attempts to work, in February 1995 she began a second cycle of homelessness, after she and her family fled the dangers of drug gangs in her public housing complex, where her apartment had been broken into and her children attacked. Once again she has joined the ranks of the nation's 3 million homeless people desperately searching for an affordable place to live. In many cities in Michigan, the wait for subsidized housing is from two to five years.

Michigan has been consistently cited as a model in discussions about how state block grants might work. Republican Governor John Engler is credited for having reduced welfare

43

"dependency." He terminated 83,000 single adults from general assistance in 1991, and cut A.F.D.C. [Aid to Families with Dependent Children] benefits to women and children by 11 percent. Hailed by the *New York Times* as the "conservative hero from the rust belt," Engler signed a seven-bill package to cut taxes and proposed spending $23 million to operate four new prisons, while simultaneously promoting further sanctions and cuts for welfare recipients. Meanwhile, poor families barely hang on. Minimum-wage jobs might proliferate, but how do you survive when the total annual income from a minimum-wage job is $8,800 a year, keeping a family of three $3,000 below the poverty line? And if you turn to welfare to survive in Michigan, A.F.D.C. payments average $435 a month, with $69 in food stamps for each family member per month. Estimates from the National Law Center on Homelessness and Poverty indicate that almost half of poor families spend up to 70 percent of their income on housing in the private market, so if you flee public housing as Deborah did, there are not many choices left; it's either living in a war zone or living on the streets.

People Want Jobs

Tanya, a working mother of two, describes her experiences in Detroit: "I lived in public housing in Detroit, I stayed there for two years, and I know the debilitating factors that it takes just to survive. People have tried and tried and tried to find jobs; it's a vicious circle and after you get the door slammed in your face, you don't have the will to go out there and fight anymore. A lot of people have given up because so much has been taken from them. It makes me really upset when they say people are sitting in front of the TV and stuff. There's people wanting jobs; when they have job fairs there's thousands of people waiting in line. People don't choose to be poor and you try to get off of welfare. You go out and work and because of one little thing or another—the worker makes a mistake or the mail doesn't get there on time—you lose what little benefits you have. People lose their A.F.D.C. or they get laid off from the job, then they become homeless, so people are just trapped."

The child care crisis compounds the situation: How do you survive as a single mother earning minimum wage and spending over 50 percent of your income on child care? In Michigan child care costs an average of $4,400 a year. According to a 1993 report of KIDS COUNT in Michigan, there were 443,000 preschool children in need of care, with only 215,000 licensed slots available. The crisis is mirrored across the nation. Reports by the Children's Defense Fund and by the Department of Health and Human Services indicate alarming deficiencies in the quality, safety and availability of federally subsidized daycare. Funding limitations tilt A.F.D.C. child care programs toward low-cost, poor-quality options well below the actual market costs of child care. So poor mothers once again are forced into impossible choices: cheap, unregulated, frequently unsafe care for their children, or no child care, or no job.

Tanya's Dilemma

Tanya highlights her own dilemma as the mother of one pre-schooler and one school-age child: "I got a little slip in my son's pocket saying I owed $900 in child care and saying don't bring my children back again until that is paid. My son's care cost $90 a week, and for my daughter after-school care cost $65 a week—I couldn't do it, so I tried to go back on A.F.D.C. It was either pay my rent or pay child care. I just couldn't pay child care expenses that got so high. So I called Social Services and asked about getting my benefits again and my worker said I had to wait two months, so I stopped work in November and she said I wouldn't get any benefits until January. I asked my worker, 'How'm I supposed to live?' and she said, 'It's not for me to tell you!'"

The desperate conditions experienced by Deborah and Tanya are shared by millions of women and children across the country—all targets of welfare reform. Under President Bill Clinton's workfare proposal, a two-years-and-you're-out-unless-you-work plan, single mothers would be held hostage to the ravages of a minimum-wage market and their children made victims of a continuing crisis in child care. The Republicans' Personal Responsibility Act—which strips the entitlement status from welfare and food assistance programs, denies cash aid to teen mothers, to children born to mothers already on welfare, to children whose paternity cannot be established, to legal immigrants, and which imposes a five-year lifetime benefit limit—simply throws poor women and children over to the states to do with "them" as they wish. [Bill Clinton vetoed the act in January 1996.] Under the present system poor families have been dropping through the gaping holes of the minimal safety net at alarming rates. What lies beyond the net?

What Single Mothers Need

Mary Ann Hinton, a mother of four and part-time worker, is an activist in her public housing complex. "You know the reason we're being attacked?" she asks angrily. "We don't have the money to fight back—they know poor people can't fight back. Why do they allow them to play games with people's lives like that? I mean, why would the American people stand for that? It's ridiculous. Look at what we're doing! You taking care of your kids, you keepin' your house clean, you sending them to school, you go looking for a job but it ain't been working out for

45

you. You gotta have at least $7 an hour to make it work, that's the least you need; cheap rent and child care and transportation—these things have to be in place for that job to work. If the government wants to do something, open up free child care centers—when your kids are young, the child care kills you."

Wasserman, ©1995, Boston Globe. Distributed by Los Angeles Times Syndicate. Reprinted with permission.

In Michigan, the centerpiece of Governor Engler's welfare reform has been work as a condition for receiving benefits. The first of Engler's trumpeted workfare innovations is something he calls the Social Contract. It requires welfare recipients (with babies over a year old) who are not in job training, working or in school to pay off their benefits by "volunteering" their unpaid labor for twenty hours per week, but neither transportation nor child care are guaranteed. Tamar Lewis, a 21-year-old mother and a community college student, explains why she refused to sign the Social Contract and risked being sanctioned: "They want you to sign promising you'll be a productive citizen. And I was a full-time student with a very good grade-point average and I was taking care of a small child. By my eyes, I was working very hard. Now for new recipients they won't pay daycare unless you work part-time *and* go to school."

Work First, Engler's coercive plan to instill the work ethic in recalcitrant recipients, requires women to work twenty hours per week *prior* to enrolling in higher education or job-training programs. Recipients are limited to only two years of college, which effectively locks them in the low-wage pink-collar ghetto. The Social Contract was cited as a model for the Personal Responsibility Act, which requires A.F.D.C. recipients to work thirty-five hours per week in "work slots" in exchange for benefits. Since the maximum A.F.D.C. grant in the median state is $366 a month for a family of three, "work slot" wages would be far below the minimum wage (approximately $2.50 an hour). Thus, most recipients will be in a state of indentured servitude. Moreover, neither child care nor exemptions for childbirth, infants and disabled children will be provided. Presumably poor mothers will give birth, and be pressed into work as their day-old infants are left alone to bottle-feed themselves, minus the WIC [Women with Infant Children]-provided formula now slated for cuts. An early initiation into self-sufficiency and personal responsibility!

All this and more lies ahead to restore the American family, "reduce welfare dependency" and avoid "the ruin of the poor." Karen Schaumann, a mother of three and a local welfare rights activist in Michigan, sums it up: "We have a right to survive, our kids have a right to survive, poor women have a right to have babies. What if we lived in a country where only wealthy people could have children? And if we have babies, they gonna take our babies away and put them in orphanages! We get $6,000 a year to live on, and orphanages cost $39,000 a year per child—where's the sense of that? There is enough money to go around in this country, there always has been, but the bottom line is there's always been poor people and there's always going to be poor people in this country until this system changes. You know those Republicans and Democrats are sitting up there in high style, high fat living in Washington. They're having $50,000-a-plate dinners—O.K., that's ten people's survival on A.F.D.C. for a year just for one dinner they eat! Where's the justice there? Who are they to tell us if you're poor, you and your kids don't have a right to survive after two years? It's a war on us—it's genocide, they want to kill us off because they don't need us as workers anymore. You know, I can compare it with Nazi Germany: They didn't start out killing all the Jewish people; they first started talking bad about them, trying to make them look evil, like they were the problem in society, and that's what's happening to us now."

False Depictions of Women

While the Republicans go about burning the bridges to survival, the Democrats are not far behind. And as their rhetoric against won't-work mothers and promiscuous teens escalates, it advances the pernicious idea that poverty is a private affair, that destitution and homelessness are simply products of bad personal choices. In this surreal world, domestic violence, a major factor in the impoverishment and homelessness of single women and children, is hardly addressed. Nor is the fact, documented by the Institute for Women's Policy Research, that 43 percent of mothers on A.F.D.C. work an average of 950 hours a year, reflecting the labor force participation of *all* working mothers in this country. Or that the majority of mothers are cyclical workers forced out of the labor market by joblessness, layoffs and critical health care and child care needs. All the women I have interviewed fit this profile, struggling to survive on part-time work and to attend job training or college. Yet as women on welfare they are depicted as passive, dependent, breeding females in need of reform. It is clear that the human rights of single mothers and their children are being decimated. If ever there was a time to join the national welfare rights struggle, it is now. As Tanya says, "The system isn't welfare, it's abuse," a belief echoed by Mary Ann Hinton, who states plainly, "They have the system made—they figured out how many of us are gonna die."

"Unwed motherhood should no longer generate entitlement to public cash aid or be perceived by teenage girls as the road to economic independence."

Single Mothers Do Not Need Welfare

George Liebmann

Prior to government assistance programs for young mothers and their families, these individuals' needs were largely met by family, friends, and charitable organizations, including maternity homes. In the following viewpoint, George Liebmann argues that unconditional government welfare checks fail to help single mothers escape poverty. Instead, he contends, privately run maternity homes can effectively assist single mothers by offering compassion and discipline, teaching responsibility, and discouraging out-of-wedlock births. Liebmann is an attorney and a former counsel to the Maryland Department of Social Services.

As you read, consider the following questions:

1. According to Liebmann, when did the Aid to Families with Dependent Children program begin?
2. In the author's opinion, what factors contributed to the decline of maternity homes?
3. Why are most out-of-wedlock births wanted by poor women, according to Liebmann?

George Liebmann, "Back to the Maternity Home," *American Enterprise*, January/February 1995. Reprinted by permission of the *American Enterprise*, a Washington, D.C.-based magazine of politics, business, and culture.

On March 18, 1993, as part of a larger effort to aid urban areas, Senator Bill Bradley proposed a nationwide network of maternity homes for young, unwed mothers—to be funded by the federal government initially to the tune of $250 million a year. These "Fifteen-Month Houses" would accommodate poor or teenage women during the last trimester of their pregnancy and the first year of their baby's life. The group homes would offer medical care, substance-abuse screening and treatment, and instruction in parenting skills. Children would be provided with nutritious food, immunizations and doctoring, and mental stimulation and care.

While this initiative was inspired by successes at recently founded maternity homes in the Bronx and Los Angeles, homes for unwed mothers are hardly new in this country. Before the government offered cash payments to unmarried mothers, hundreds of private maternity homes provided vital services in every major city. These important institutions cared for tens of thousands of endangered women and children by building confidence, inculcating healthy new habits, actively discouraging illegitimacy, and working to integrate endangered families back into mainstream society.

There is nothing whatever to prevent maternity homes from carrying out these same useful tasks today. We need only set the stage—and then stop subsidizing the alternatives.

The Crittenton Homes

Before about 1915, there was no government aid at all for unwed mothers. Because an out-of-wedlock birth would bring a woman both serious economic hardship and community disapproval, such events were quite rare (comprising fewer than 4 percent of all births). There *were* provisions for women in crisis, however, in the form of an extensive network of private maternity homes. In Cleveland in 1925, for example, various groups ran five such residences, which between them served nearly all the unwed mothers in the city.

Some of the most prominent maternity homes were the Florence Crittenton Homes, which existed in numerous locations across the country. These have been the subject of several books, and the evidence shows they were generally quite successful in their humane missions. The Crittenton Homes shielded mothers from psychological or material worries during and after their confinement; they provided nutritional and medical services that encouraged healthy deliveries; they helped stressed individuals become better prepared to mother; and for women who lacked the means or capacity to raise their babies themselves, they helped arrange adoptions. These homes also sought to ensure, through moral and religious teaching, that an unmarried mother

50

did not bear further children out of wedlock.

In 1971, scholar Prudence Rains found the surviving Crittenton Homes to be fascinating examples of institutions in which rehabilitation, not just physical maintenance, was the main undertaking. During their period of residence, many maternity home clients experience what "could be described as conversion," according to Rains. The average stay at a Crittenton Home was 20 months, and, in the end, 60 percent of the mothers chose to place their children up for adoption.

Maternity homes have by no means disappeared from the national scene. But it's true that most of those that existed prior to World War II were squeezed out of existence—despite their many benefits to hard-pressed women, endangered children, and society as a whole—by the vast growth of direct government payments to unwed mothers. In this, maternity homes were victims of a tragic error in social policy.

Money Alone Is Not the Answer

For most of American history, social workers and others who work with the poor have maintained that money is not what members of the underclass need most. In the early decades of the twentieth century, providers of social aid "held as a fundamental principle that financial aid was a very minor, if not negligible element of family rehabilitation," notes R. Lubove.

Indeed, charitable activists warned, simply giving the poor funds could actually make things worse. It would "be obnoxious and injurious, would cultivate the pauper spirit, would increase pauperism, parasitism, and dependence" to hand cash to individual families, the New York Commission on Relief for Widowed Mothers cautioned in 1914. "To pension desertion or illegitimacy would, undoubtedly, have the effect of a premium on these crimes against society," stated Homer Folks. Reformers emphasized the moral roots of pauperism, and took the view that it would be, as the National Conference of Charities and Corrections argued in 1912, "a dangerous experiment [to try] to solve social problems by merely giving money."

Until enactment of the Aid to Families with Dependent Children (AFDC) program in 1935, the financial and other needs of unwed mothers in America were handled either by friends and relatives or "on a relatively ad hoc basis relying in large part on private referrals and organization in the sphere of women," notes J.J. Brumberg. Private social services were built on "empathy, a sense of community responsibility, class orientation, religious fervor, and awareness of the double standard and knowledge of the exigencies of economic life for unmarried women," Brumberg reports.

In the welfare-less society, aid to women facing crisis pregnancies was centered in local maternity homes offering shelter, the company of peers, and the care of compassionate stewards. This local lattice of maternity homes began to fall apart only when the AFDC program was set up by the Franklin Delano Roosevelt administration in 1935. And that damage was largely unintended.

During the mid-1930s, there were approximately 227,000 recipients of state mothers' pensions—virtually none of whom were parents of illegitimate children. The new AFDC legislation, however, quietly provided payments to unwed mothers on the same terms as widowed and abandoned mothers. This extension of cash aid to cover illegitimacy was basically a policy accident; a small cabal of bureaucrats engineered the plan without the participation of the responsible cabinet officer, Secretary of Labor Frances Perkins. By the time Perkins discovered what she had wrought, it was too late to do anything about it, to her dismay. "She felt the Children's Bureau let her down on the provision," reports biographer G.D. Reilly.

> She always thought a "dependent mother" was a widow with small children or one whose children had been disabled in an industrial accident or one who married a ne'er-do-well who had deserted her or hit the bottle. She said it never occurred to her, in view of the fact that she'd been active in drives for homes that took care of mothers with illegitimate children, that these mothers would be called "dependent" in the new legislation. She blamed the huge illegitimacy rates among blacks on aid to mothers with dependent children.

Within two years of AFDC's enactment, the number of individuals receiving government public assistance had more than doubled, including lots of unmarried mothers. Maternity homes went into eclipse. Institutions that expected behavioral reform could not compete with no-strings checks. Though some maternity homes sought to get the new AFDC disbursements channeled through their institutions instead of going directly to individuals (particularly in the case of very young mothers), no sufficient amount of AFDC aid ever flowed through the homes. Part of the problem was that as the 1930s and 1940s unfolded, social workers exhibited growing hostility toward maternity homes—primarily because of their moral and religious principles. "Many social workers believed that institutional treatment in maternity homes was incompatible with the 'individualized' therapeutic approach and ignored the similarities between this approach and the older one of individual reclamation," reports scholar M.J. Morton.

Thoughtless program rules, the lazy lure of simply offering checks instead of personal assistance, and a measure of ideological hostility toward private charitable relief among a thin but influential slice of the therapeutic community all combined fatally against maternity homes. Not coincidentally, unwed motherhood began its long climb to prominence at the same time.

Family and Group Assistance

It is time we fixed the error that worried Frances Perkins in 1935. Unwed motherhood should no longer generate entitlement to public cash aid or be perceived by teenage girls as the road to economic independence. Rather, as the timid 1988 welfare amendments began to suggest, young unwed mothers should receive their primary assistance from their own families, where extant, and from private group homes subsidized with public funds where family assistance is unavailable. Private maternity homes are currently experiencing a small renaissance, with new homes being established and existing homes expanding. This growth can and should be multiplied many fold.

Young unwed mothers as a class should be viewed as persons peculiarly in need of supervision, education, discipline, and reform, and not as appropriate beneficiaries of unconditional cash payments. Group homes can play an extremely useful role in this area. They are a way for communities to provide care in the critical months before and after birth, and to instruct new mothers in child care and the responsibilities of parenting. They can assist placements for adoption. And they can be the means by which the community discourages further out-of-wedlock births.

With all that in mind, the following program ought to be pursued:

Cash welfare benefits should be ended immediately for all new unwed mothers, who should instead receive, as an entitlement, group home care of a specified duration. After their period in residence, beneficiaries should receive supervision of their independent living arrangements. They should be offered easy access to counseling and social services. Mutual aid in the provision of child care should be promoted.

Since passage of the 1988 AFDC amendments, states have been allowed to disburse their aid to teenage unwed mothers in this form. But none has taken the initiative. It is time now to seize that opportunity and also to extend the same principle to mothers older than 18.

It will not work to fund maternity homes as a kind of add-on. Governments must simultaneously stop providing beneficiaries with other easier paths. Maternity homes, with the demands they place on their residents, will only root deeply if the alternative of responsibility-free cash payments is no longer available to women who bear children they cannot support. To provide for all new aid applicants from now on, funds previously appropriated for AFDC and food stamps should instead be channeled through group homes. This would assure adequate support for infants born out of wedlock, while simultaneously ending the liberating economic subsidies that illegitimate birth currently brings young women and their men.

Reviving Maternity Homes

America's new maternity homes should in no event become governmentally operated. Instead, as Senator Bradley proposed, there should be a substantial program of capital grants (akin to Hill-Burton payments to private hospitals) to foster new maternity homes run by voluntary agencies. And there should be no restriction with respect to religious content of programs so long as basic services are provided. All clients, after all, will enroll themselves voluntarily and choose their own homes.

In the 103rd Congress, Representative Chris Smith of New Jersey introduced a bill that aimed to assist the growth of new homes without stifling them under the regulations and attached strings that often accompany government money. It proposed to distribute vouchers to individuals rather than supporting institutions: "A bill to directly . . . establish a program to provide pregnant women with certificates to cover expenses incurred in receiving services at maternity and housing services facilities. . . ." Just as government payments made to individuals can and do flow through religious hospitals, daycare centers, and universities, so too could a wide range of maternity homes qualify and compete for clients. (The Smith bill also had a provision directing the secretary of Housing and Urban Development to help nonprofit entities of all sorts obtain and rehabilitate vacant government buildings for use as maternity homes.)

When clients leave maternity homes after perhaps a year or two of supervised residence, they should have access, in lieu of cash payments, to new federal per capita grants funding social services for unwed mothers. These social services should again be delivered via the voluntary, not the government, sector. In effect, each unwed mother would have an expense account she could cash in for private counseling, training, and services. Food stamps should remain an entitlement as at present, since unwed motherhood is not a condition of eligibility for them. It should be possible, however, to direct these payments to a maternity home or designated guardian in appropriate cases, instead of always paying them to an individual.

State Measures

Even in the absence of federal action, there is much states can do on their own. Any state could immediately pass a law akin to the Pregnancy Freedom of Choice Act in California, which provides for public payment of the full cost of maternity home care for at least six weeks preceding and six weeks following birth.

Such measures would cost no more than $2,000–$3,000 per recipient above the currently available AFDC, food stamp, and Medicaid benefits for a three-month confinement, and the benefits would include improved prenatal and postnatal care, provision of adoption services, education in birth control methods not conflicting with the mother's religious precepts, assistance in formulating education and work plans, and discouragement of further out-of-wedlock births. The California legislation and measures in other states that provide outpatient counseling to pregnant mothers suggest that this is one area of policy in which the groups passionately favoring and opposing abortion can reach some agreement. (In any case, it is clear that abortion on demand offers no solution to our welfare problem. Twenty years of rising out-of-wedlock birthrates in the face of liberalized abortion laws demonstrate that. Whether a particular conception was intended or not, research indicates that most births out of wedlock among underclass women today are "wanted"— because motherhood creates entitlements.)

Current American welfare policy is plagued by an ideology of cash entitlement. What the poor really need today is not a check but a powerful set of rehabilitative social services. These should be offered by private community groups, without any illusion of moral neutrality. Rescuing an underclass is by definition a highly moralistic undertaking, and one that requires rescuers possessing equal measures of confidence, compassion, and personal knowledge of the people they are helping.

Although these suggestions may be unfamiliar—even jarring—to some readers, many are already partially accepted by statute. Let those with knee-jerk critical responses justify continuation of our current colossal failures. Let them respond, preferably after a visit to one of the maternity homes operating today, with better alternatives. Let critics who regard these suggestions as paternalistic reflect on the fact that they relate to the redirection of men and women who in many cases operate beyond the boundaries of wholesome society, individuals who are producing frightfully neglected children while they are still children themselves, individuals who have received hardly any direction or training through conventional cultural channels. Let readers who think these proposals harsh consider the fallout of our last 30 years of welfare practice reflected in rates of illegitimate birth, child abuse, repeat abortion, and juvenile crime. Perhaps they will forgive the author's skepticism that wider distribution of monthly checks and condoms is all that is needed.

And perhaps they will come to favor an already-tried and well-proven approach for addressing one of the nation's most overwhelming problems.

"Private charities can do a better job than government."

Charitable Aid Should Replace Government Welfare

Marvin Olasky

In the following viewpoint, Marvin Olasky argues that before the advent of government welfare programs, America's private and religious charities met the needs of the poor. In fact, he maintains, unlike the current welfare system, these charities were successful in reducing dependence and helping people work their way out of poverty. America's welfare system, Olasky asserts, should be replaced with a network of charitable organizations that would care for the poor by stressing the importance of family bonds, employment, and spiritual guidance. Olasky is a senior fellow at the Progress and Freedom Foundation, a public policy research center in Washington, D.C.

As you read, consider the following questions:

1. What was the rate of out-of-wedlock births in 1995, according to Olasky?
2. According to Olasky, what are "work tests"?
3. In the author's opinion, why is giving, by itself, inadequate?

Marvin Olasky, "The New Welfare Debate: How to Practice Effective Compassion," *Imprimis*, September 1995. Reprinted by permission of *Imprimis*, a publication of Hillsdale College, Hillsdale, Michigan.

For too long the welfare debate has been the "same old same old." Liberals have emphasized distribution of bread and assumed the poor could live on that alone. Conservatives have complained about the mold on the bread and pointed out the waylaying of funds by "welfare queens" and the empire-building of "poverty pimps."

It is time now, however, to talk not about reforming the welfare system—which often means scraping off a bit of mold—but about replacing it with a revolutionary, centrist system based on private and religious charity. Such a system was effective in the nineteenth century and will be even more effective in the twenty-first century, with the decentralization that new technology makes possible. But we must also make the right changes in personal goals and public policy.

Replacing Welfare

Why is welfare replacement necessary? Because in America we now face not just concern about poor individuals falling between the cracks, but the crunch of sidewalks disintegrating. An explosive growth in the number of children born out of wedlock—in 1995, one of every three of our fellow citizens is beginning life hindered by the absence of a father—is one indication of rapid decline.

Why is welfare replacement politically possible? Because there is broad understanding that the system hurts the very people it was designed to help, and that the trillions of dollars spent in the name of compassion over the past three decades have largely been wasted. Conservatives who want an opportunity to recover past wisdom and apply it to future practice should thank liberals for providing a wrecked ship. And liberals should support welfare replacement because, given the mood of the country, the alternative to replacement is not an expanded welfare state, but an extinct one.

Why is welfare replacement morally right? Because, when we look at the present system, we are dealing with not just the dispersal of dollars but with the destruction of lives. When William Tecumseh Sherman's army marched through Georgia in 1864, about 25,000 blacks followed his infantry columns, until Sherman and his soldiers decided to rid themselves of the followers by hurrying across an unfordable stream and then taking up the pontoon bridge, leaving the ex-slaves stranded on the opposite bank. Many tried to swim across but died in the icy water. Similarly today, many of the stranded poor will soon be abandoned by a country that has seen welfare failure and is lapsing into a skeptical and even cynical "compassion syndrome"—unless we find a way to renew the American dream of compassion.

The destruction of life through the current welfare system is not often so dramatic, but the death of dreams is evident every day. During the past three decades, we have seen lives destroyed and dreams die among poor individuals who have gradually become used to dependency. Those who stressed independence used to be called the "worthy poor"; now, a person who will not work is also worthy, and mass pauperism is accepted. Now, those who are willing to put off immediate gratification and to sacrifice leisure time in order to remain independent are called chumps rather than champs.

We have also seen dreams die among some social workers who had been in the forefront of change. Their common lament is, "All we have time to do is move paper." Those who really care do not last long, and one who resigned cried out, "I had a calling; it was that simple. I wanted to help." Some social workers take satisfaction in meeting demands, but others who want to change lives become despondent in their role of enabling destructive behavior.

We have seen dreams die as "compassion fatigue" deepens. Personal involvement is down, cynicism is up. Many of us would like to be generous at the subway entrance or the street corner, but we know that most homeless recipients will use any available funds for drugs or alcohol. We end up walking by, avoiding eye contact—and a subtle hardening occurs once more. Many of us would like to contribute more of our money and time to the poor, but we are weighed down by heavy tax burdens. We end up just saying "no" to personal involvement, and a sapping of citizenship occurs once more.

We have seen dreams die among children who will never know their fathers. Government welfare programs have contributed to the removal of fathers, and nothing can replace them.

Some would say that for the poor and the fatherless the death of dreams is inevitable, but that is not so. England in the nineteenth century recovered from its downward spiral that began in the eighteenth century. And we in the United States in the twenty-first century can recover from our recent problems, since we know a great deal from our own experience about how to fight poverty. We had successful anti-poverty programs a century ago—successful because they embodied personal, material, and spiritual involvement and challenge.

A Successful War on Poverty

This vital story has generally been ignored by liberal historians, but the documented history goes like this: During the nineteenth century, a successful war on poverty was waged by tens of thousands of local, private charitable agencies and religious groups around the country. The platoons of the greatest charity army in American history often were small. They were made up of volunteers led by poorly paid but deeply dedicated professional managers. And they were highly effective.

Thousands of eyewitness accounts and journalistic assessments show that poverty fighters of the nineteenth century did not abolish poverty, but they enabled millions of people to escape it. They saw springs of fresh water flowing among the poor, not just blocks of ice sitting in a perpetual winter of multigenerational welfare dependency. And the optimism prevalent then contrasts sharply with the demoralization among the poor and the cynicism among the better-off that is so common now.

What was their secret? It was not neglect. It was their understanding of the literal and biblical meaning of compassion, which comes from two Latin words—*com*, which means "with," and *pati*, which means "to suffer." The word points to personal involvement with the needy, suffering with them, not just giving to them. "Suffering with" means adopting hard-to-place babies, providing shelter to women undergoing crisis pregnancies, becoming a big brother to a fatherless child, working one-on-one with a young single mother. It is not easy—but it works.

Our predecessors did not have it easy—but they persevered. Theirs were not "the good old days." Work days were long and affluence was rare, and homes on the average were much smaller than ours. There were severe drug and alcohol problems and many more early deaths from disease. We are more spread out now, but our travel time is not any greater. Overall, most of the problems paralleled our own; the big difference lies in the rates of increase in illegitimacy and divorce. Most of the opportunities and reasons to help also were similar; a big difference in this regard is, as I have already pointed out, that our tax burden is much larger, and many Americans justifiably feel that they are already paying for others to take care of the needy.

In the nineteenth century, volunteers opened their own homes to deserted women and orphaned children. They offered employment to nomadic men who had abandoned hope and most human contact. Most significantly, our predecessors made moral demands on recipients of aid. They saw family, work, freedom, and faith as central to our being, not as "lifestyle options." The volunteers gave of their own lives not just so that others might survive, but that they might thrive.

Principles of Effective Compassion

Affiliation. A century ago, when individuals applied for material assistance, charity volunteers tried first to "restore family ties that have been sundered" and "reabsorb in social life those who for some reason have snapped the threads that bound them to other members of the community." Instead of immediately offering help, charities asked, "Who is bound to help in this case?" In 1897, Mary Richmond of the Baltimore Charity Organizing Society summed up the wisdom of a century: "Relief given without reference to friends and neighbors is accompanied by moral loss. Poor neighborhoods are doomed to grow poorer whenever the natural ties of neighborliness are weakened by well-meant but unintelligent interference."

Today, before developing a foundation project or contributing to a private charity, we should ask, "Does it work through families, neighbors, and religious or community organizations, or does it supersede them?" For example, studies show that many homeless alcoholics have families, but they do not want to be with them. When homeless shelters provide food, clothing, and housing without asking hard questions, aren't they subsidizing disaffiliation and enabling addiction? Instead of giving aid directly to homeless men, why not work on reuniting them with brothers, sisters, parents, wives, or children?

A Charitable Approach to Welfare

An ideal welfare system is one that helps people in genuine need, without at the same time encouraging antisocial behavior. This ideal has never been achieved through large bureaucratic federal welfare programs. But the reduced size, greater flexibility and hands-on management style that distinguishes many private-sector charities permits them to monitor behavior and incorporate innovative methods for helping the poor.

Merrill Matthews Jr., *Washington Times*, February 24, 1995.

We should ask as well whether other programs help or hurt. It is good to help an unmarried teenage mother, but much of such aid now offers a mirage of independence. A better plan is to reunite her whenever possible with those on whom she actually depends, whether she admits it or not: her parents and the child's father. It is good to give Christmas presents to poor children, but when the sweet-minded "helper" shows up with a shiny new fire truck that outshines the second-hand items a poor single mom put together, the damage is done. A better plan is to bulwark the beleaguered mom by enabling her to provide for her children.

Bonding. A century ago, when applicants for help were truly alone, volunteers worked one-to-one to become, in essence, new family members. Charity volunteers a century ago usually were not assigned to massive food-dispensing tasks. They were given the narrow but deep responsibility of making a difference in one life over several years. Kindness and firmness were both

60

essential. In 1898, the magazine *American Hebrew* told of how one man was sunk into dependency but a volunteer "with great patience convinced him that he must earn his living." Soon he did, and he regained the respect of his family and community. Similarly, a woman had become demoralized, but "for months she was worked with, now through kindness, again through discipline, until finally she began to show a desire to help herself."

Today, when an unmarried pregnant teenager is dumped by her boyfriend and abandoned by angry parents who refuse to be reconciled, she needs a haven, a room in a home with a volunteer family. When a single mom at the end of her rope cannot take care of a toddler, he should be placed quickly for adoption where a new and permanent bonding can take place, rather than rotated through a succession of foster homes.

Work Tests

Categorization. A century ago, charities realized that two persons in exactly the same material circumstances but with different values need different treatment: One might benefit most from some material help and a pat on the back; the other might need spiritual challenge and a push. Those who were orphaned, elderly, or disabled received aid. Jobless adults who were "able and willing to work" received help in job-finding. Those who preferred "to live on alms" and those of "confirmed intemperance" were not entitled to material assistance.

"Work tests" helped both in sorting and in providing relief with dignity. When an able-bodied man came to a homeless shelter, he often was asked to chop wood for two hours or whitewash a building; in that way he could provide part of his own support and also help those unable to perform these chores. A needy woman generally was given a seat in the "sewing room" (often near a child care room) and asked to work on garments that would be donated to the helpless poor or sent through the Red Cross to families suffering from the effects of hurricanes, floods, or other natural disasters. The work test, along with teaching good habits and keeping away those who did not really need help, also enabled charities to teach the lesson that those who were being helped could help others.

Today, we need to stop talking about "the poor" in abstraction and start distinguishing once again between those who truly yearn for help and those who just want an enabler. Programs have the chance to succeed only when categories are established and firmly maintained. Work tests can help: Why shouldn't some homeless men clean up streets and parks and remove graffiti? Now, thousands of crack babies (born addicted to cocaine and often deserted by mothers who care only for the next high) languish in hospitals and shelters under bright lights with almost no human contact. Shouldn't homeless women (those who are healthy and gentle) be assigned to hold a baby for an hour in exchange for food and shelter?

Discernment. "Intelligent giving and intelligent withholding are alike true charity," the New Orleans Charity Organization Society declared in 1899. It added, "If drink has made a man poor, money will feed not him, but his drunkenness." Poverty-fighters a century ago trained volunteers to leave behind "a conventional attitude toward the poor, seeing them through the comfortable haze of our own intentions." Barriers against fraud were important not only to prevent waste but to preserve morale among those who *were* working hard to remain independent: "Nothing," declared the Society, "is more demoralizing to the struggling poor than successes of the indolent."

Bad charity also created uncertainty among givers as to how their contributions would be used and thus led to less giving over the long term. It was important to "reform those mild, well-meaning, tender-hearted, sweet-voiced criminals who insist upon indulging in indiscriminate charity." Compassion was greatest when givers could "work with safety, confidence, and liberty." Today, lack of discernment in helping poor individuals is rapidly producing an anti-compassion backlash, as the better-off, unable to distinguish between the truly needy and the "grubby-grabby," give to neither.

New Emphasis

Employment. Nineteenth-century New York charity leader Josephine Lowell wrote that "the problem before those who would be charitable is not how to deal with a given number of the poor; it is how to help those who are poor without adding to their numbers and constantly increasing the evils they seek to cure." If people were paid for not working, the number of non-workers would increase, and children would grow up without seeing work as a natural and essential part of life. Individuals had to accept responsibility: Governmental programs operating without the discipline of the marketplace were inherently flawed, because their payout came "from what is regarded as a practically inexhaustible source, and people who once receive it are likely to regard it as a right, as a permanent pension, implying no obligation on their part."

In the twentieth century and beyond, programs that stress employment, sometimes in creative ways, need new emphasis. For example, instead of temporary housing, more of the able-bodied might receive the opportunity to work for a permanent home through "sweat equity" arrangements in which labor constitutes most of the down payment. Some who start in rigorous programs of this sort drop out with complaints that too much sweat is required, but one person who stayed in such a program said at the end, "We are poor, but we have something that is ours. When you use your own blood, sweat, and tears, it's part of your soul. You stand and say, 'I did it.'"

Freedom. Charity workers a century ago did not press for governmental programs, but instead showed poor people how to move up while resisting enslavement to governmental masters. Job freedom was the opportunity to drive a wagon without paying bribes, to cut hair without having to go to barber college, and to get a foot on the lowest rung of the ladder, even if wages there were low. Freedom was the opportunity for a family to escape dire poverty by having a father work long hours and a mother sew garments at home. Life was hard, but static, multi-generational poverty of the kind we now have was rare; those who persevered could star in a motion picture of upward mobility.

Today, in our desire to make the bottom rung of the economic ladder higher, we have cut off the lowest rungs and left many on the ground. Those who are pounding the pavements looking for work, and those who have fallen between the cracks, are hindered by what is supposed to help them. Mother Teresa's plan to open a homeless shelter in New York was stopped by a building code that required an elevator; nuns in her order said that they would carry upstairs anyone who could not walk, but the city stuck to its guns and the shelter never opened. In Texas and New Mexico, a Bible-based anti-drug program run by Victory Fellowship has a 60 percent success rate in beating addiction, yet the Commission on Drug and Alcohol Abuse has instructed the program to stop calling itself one of "drug rehabilitation" because it does not conform to bureaucratic standards.

Spiritual Needs

God. "True philanthropy must take into account spiritual as well as physical needs," poverty-fighters a century ago noted, and both Christians and Jews did. Bible-believing Christians worshiped a God who came to earth and showed in life and death the literal meaning of compassion—*suffering with.* Jewish teaching stressed the pursuit of righteousness through the doing of good deeds. Groups such as the Industrial Christian Alliance noted that they used "religious methods"—reminding the poor that God made them and had high expectations for them—to "restore the fallen and helpless to self-respect and self-support."

Today, the challenge that goes beyond the material is still essential to poverty-fighting. In Washington, D.C., multimillion-dollar programs have failed, but, a mile from the U.S. Capitol, success stories are developing: spiritually-based programs such as Clean and Sober Streets, where ex-alcoholics and ex-addicts help those still in captivity; the Gospel Mission, which fights homelessness by offering true hope; and the Capitol Hill Crisis Pregnancy Center, where teenage moms and their born and unborn children are cared for. They are all saving lives. In Dallas, Texas, a half-mile from the Dallas Housing Authority's failed projects, a neighborhood group called Voice of Hope invites teenagers to learn about God through Bible studies and to work at remodeling deteriorated homes in their neighborhood. During the past decade, crime rates among the boys involved with Voice of Hope and pregnancy rates among the girls have been dramatically lower than those in the surrounding community.

Private Charities Can Do the Job

We need to change our methods of fighting poverty, but we need to be clear about the reasons for change. Government welfare programs should be replaced not because they are too expensive—although, clearly, much money is wasted—but because they are inevitably too stingy in providing what is truly important: the treatment of people as human beings made in God's image, not as animals to be fed and caged.

Private charities can do a better job than government, but only if they practice the principles of effective compassion. *Giving*, by itself, we need to remember, is morally neutral. We need to give *rightly*, so as not to impede the development of values that enable people to get out of poverty and stay out. Only when the seven principles of effective compassion noted above are widely understood and practiced can anti-poverty work succeed. In 1995, as in 1895, the best programs offer challenge, not just enabling, and they deal with spiritual questions as well as material needs. In 1995, as in 1895, there is no effective substitute for the hard process of one person helping another. And the century-old question—Does any given "scheme of help . . . make great demands on men to give themselves to their brethren?"—is still the right one to ask.

"Few churches and charities . . . have the private income necessary to provide [welfare support] to poor families in any number."

Charitable Aid Cannot Replace Government Welfare

Fred Kammer

Many charities rely on some form of government funding to operate. In the following viewpoint, Fred Kammer argues that few charities receive sufficient private donations to survive without additional aid from the government. The government has a responsibility to help needy citizens, Kammer maintains, and only the government has the resource capacity to meet the poor's basic needs. The partnership between charities and government is the ideal means to help the poor, he asserts. Kammer is a Jesuit priest and the president of Catholic Charities USA.

As you read, consider the following questions:

1. How many Americans live in poverty, according to Kammer?
2. According to the author, what are the conservative and liberal criticisms of the government-religious charities relationship?
3. In Kammer's opinion, why did many states fail to participate in the 1988 Welfare Reform Act?

Fred Kammer, "Compassion Alone Won't Do the Job," *Insight*, April 3–10, 1995. Reprinted by permission from *Insight*. Copyright 1995, The Washington Times Corporation. All rights reserved.

I recently spent an evening at Christ House, an Alexandria, Va., homeless shelter and soup kitchen sponsored by Catholic Charities of the Diocese of Arlington County, Va. In my travels across the country, I often witness the wonderful work of some of the 272,000 staff members and volunteers who make Catholic Charities the nation's largest voluntary social service network.

On that evening, I spent most of my time talking with two shelter residents. Both men had come on hard times, one from the economy and the other from a job-related injury. Both rose early for nearly minimum-wage work, were saving money for their own apartments (Christ House has a five-week maximum stay), were in debt and found it hard to make ends meet. But they were grateful for Christ House.

Christ House is made possible by church, private and United Way funding. It receives one small government grant—less than 2 percent of its budget. Forming the backbone of its soup kitchen are 1,600 volunteers who prepare and serve 35,000 meals a year. It is a wonderful program reflecting the best combination of community, church and, yes, some government funds.

Catholic Charities of Arlington has another program in Alexandria, the Martin de Porres Center. There, older adults receive meals, education and social services. From the center, outreach takes place to homebound elders, many of whom live on Social Security, supplemental security income, or SSI, and food stamps. Nearly 30 percent of the center's funds come from the Older Americans Act.

Both the Martin de Porres Center and Christ House have numerous volunteers and United Way support and are considered model community programs. That one has 30 percent government funding and the other 2 percent does not distinguish the quality of care provided.

Lacking Private Income

Few churches and charities, in fact, have the private income necessary to provide long-term housing, social services and, especially, steady income support to poor families in any number. That is a role government has played since the 1930s, when the Great Depression ended the illusion that private charity could maintain millions of poor people in decent living conditions reflective of human dignity. Now we live in a post-depression economic system where unemployment and underemployment regularly leave 30 million Americans with incomes—if any—below the poverty line.

Government plays two primary roles for such families. First, federal or state governments provide income directly through insurance or welfare programs. Included are Social Security, SSI for low-income people who are elderly or disabled, Aid to Families

With Dependent Children, or AFDC, and veterans benefits. Often, when government wants to deliver services—such as child group homes, refugee resettlement or job training—instead of income, it works with experienced social service organizations.

Charities Need Government Funding

Most private charities depend heavily on government money, awarded through a combination of contracts and grants. The Forest Hills Community House [in New York], for example, draws $2.1 million of its $3 million budget—or 70 percent—from government financing.

Even big national charities rely on government aid. In 1994, Catholic Charities USA, a network of about 1,400 social service agencies, received about $1.3 billion, or two-thirds of its revenues, from federal, state and local governments.

The Salvation Army draws about 17 percent of its revenue from government nationally, although in some areas the figure is 66 percent, or higher, said Raymond Peacock, a lieutenant colonel in the group. He calls a government role necessary.

"This is more than a private charity responsibility," he said. "It is a societal responsibility. We can address some of it alone, but we cannot address all of it."

Karen W. Arenson, *San Diego Union-Tribune*, June 4, 1995.

In such programs, churches and charities play a different role than in many emergency services. Here, governments at the federal, state and local levels contract with charities to provide specialized services to affected groups. This "purchase of service" has been an essential part of government's approach to social needs for much of the twentieth century. Just as the federal government pays Lockheed to build an airplane or IBM to design a computer, it pays human-service providers, usually after competitive bidding, to provide specialized social services and care. An example would be foster-home care for infants with fetal alcohol syndrome.

An Effective Partnership

Catholic Charities agencies are proud to help people in need. It is our mission as church, as charity and as partner with community, business and government. We view our partnership with government like our participation in the United Way: helping us to meet community needs in an effective and efficient way.

Government contracts with us—as it does with the Salvation

Army, Lutheran Social Services, the Council of Jewish Federations and hundreds of local religious charities—because it knows we are community-based, trusted by those we serve and scrupulous about stewardship of our resources. Governments often seek us out to deliver these services because they trust us to do the job right. We also have to be vigilant that funding by government, like United Way, foundations and individual donors, does not cause us to abandon the values that undergird this compassionate work.

Hundreds of local agency boards decide to contract with government so they can contribute to the common good and to government's responsibility "to promote the general welfare" as provided for in the preamble to the Constitution. We bring our concern for people, values, experience, volunteers and private funding to make this partnership effective. (Often, governments require a financial "match" for their contracts.) We also recognize that our private dollars stretch public dollars and allow much, much more to be done than either could accomplish alone.

Both government and religious charities then see the relationship as a partnership that helps each to be faithful to its own mission. These relationships are not without their problems, which are typical for the public-private partnerships about which we hear so much these days.

Critics of the Partnership

Recently, critics have challenged such partnerships in human and social services. On the extreme left, church-state separatists want religious charities as far away from public programs as possible. They don't want us to bring our values of human dignity, community and ethical standards to bear on services. On the far right come those who see government money as somehow "corrupting" our religious mission and religious giving. They argue that charity will be purer and more generous if government were not involved.

Ironically, these same voices on the extreme right also argue that charities—from whom they would strip all government funding—will pick up the slack if the Congress slashes both income support and social services.

The argument about government money driving out private charity is just that: an argument. Proponents produce no studies, no experiments, no proof. It is, at best, sociological speculation fueled by ideological wishfulness. If it were just speculation, think-tank theories or armchair theology, it could go unchallenged. However, supporters propose to risk the lives, health and futures of low-income families on their hunches. They feel free to do so, because it will cost them nothing to throw people in need to the vagaries of private charity. I wish they were willing to put their own children's futures or the care of their elderly parents to the same test.

Donors and Volunteers

Certainly, I know of churches and individuals who excuse their lack of concern for poor families by saying that government or United Way or some charity will do the job. But I also know that despite the fact that Catholic Charities receives two-thirds of its funding from governments, we also have wonderful donors and volunteers and expect to have many more in the future. While our government partnership has grown during the last 20 years, so too has our private giving and volunteering. In 1973, our agencies reported $139 million from nongovernment sources to support their programs. By 1993, that total had risen to $620 million. In 1981, our members reported 20,000 volunteers; in 1993, that number had grown tenfold to more than 200,000.

So while critics on the right contend that government funding will drive out private dollars and volunteers, that is not our experience. Even where government monies are far greater than in Alexandria, I find wonderful volunteers, donors and local boards working to make sure that all services, however funded, are high in quality and deeply caring.

Frankly, if the cuts proposed in the House Personal Responsibility Act were passed, we could not fill the gaps slashed in the nation's safety net. Charities certainly can do more with the help of volunteers and donors. But the government—"we the people"—should not do less.

This is not just my personal opinion. It is the considered judgment of experienced Catholic Charities leaders across this nation, echoed by the Salvation Army, the St. Vincent de Paul Society, the Council of Jewish Federations, Second Harvest, Feed the Children, Lutheran Social Services and many others. The people we serve and our services for them will be devastated.

Struggling to Meet Needs

In 1993, Catholic Charities served 10.6 million people of every social, economic, ethnic and religious background. Nearly 7 million people came to us for emergency services—primarily food and shelter. That includes 1.7 million children.

Our agencies constantly are struggling to meet the basic needs of people. We should be providing more services that help people regain self-sufficiency. Instead, since 1983 we have been forced by government cuts and the economy into the emergency food and shelter business. In 1994, we provided emergency services to about two-thirds of those we served. Compare that with the situation in 1983, when only one-fourth needed food or shelter.

Instead of using resources to help people overcome obstacles such as joblessness or alcoholism, we face working families who come to us for food when their minimum-wage paychecks won't last the week. And we provide hot meals to too many people who cannot find jobs and cannot make ends meet with government benefits.

We believe that only government has the resource capacity—not to mention the political and moral responsibility—to promote the general welfare. That begins with life-sustaining food and nutrition and includes basic income supports for those who cannot work.

Private charities work in partnership with the government. As church and as charity, we cannot fulfill the government's role in feeding hungry people or meeting needs for basic income. Even with increased giving—with or without new tax credits—we do not have the means to make up for a proposed $60 billion in budget cuts or $18 billion in cuts in food programs. We already serve 700 percent more people with emergency services than in 1981. Compare the proposed cuts, for example, with the fact that the entire national United Way effort only raises $3 billion-plus a year.

States' Shaky Record

We hear a lot of talk these days about turning programs over to the states. Sadly, the historical record raises profound doubts about the will or ability of states to protect our poorest families from the ravages of hunger and poverty. I write this as a Southerner who worked for years in Louisiana and Georgia and watched state legislatures firsthand. Despite recent political promises of a few governors, we should keep in mind the following points:

- State reforms are as yet untested and unproven in making significant improvements in welfare programs.
- As a national average, states have allowed AFDC benefits per family to decline steadily for decades.
- Many state systems of care for abused and neglected children have failed miserably and been taken over by the courts. Nationally, 100 children died in 1994 in state foster-care and child-care systems.
- Many states failed to avail themselves of the 1988 Welfare Reform Act's provisions for moving parents from welfare to work because they were unable or unwilling to put in their share of funding.
- States often have been punitive toward poor families.

The fact that food-stamp benefits increase when AFDC declines is one further reason not to turn the food programs over to state politics where they no longer will be the refuge of last resort for hungry poor families.

Federal food programs have reflected the determination of Congress that in the world's most powerful nation, children and families will not starve to death. Now, when poverty is at one of its highest levels in decades, that commitment should not change.

Jesus Christ could feed 5,000 people with a few loaves of bread and fish and, while we may try the same, it is neither sound social policy nor responsible government to put people's lives in jeopardy in hope of miracles. While there are promises that church people will come out to meet new needs created by congressional neglect, the poor already are lined up at our shelters and sometimes turned away from our overwhelmed services.

Periodical Bibliography

The following articles have been selected to supplement the diverse views presented in this chapter. Addresses are provided for periodicals not indexed in the *Readers' Guide to Periodical Literature*, the *Alternative Press Index*, or the *Social Sciences Index*.

American Enterprise	Special section on welfare, January/February 1995.
David T. Beito	"Poor Before Welfare," *National Review*, May 6, 1996.
Douglas J. Besharov	"Welfare Reform Without Illusions," *Washington Post National Weekly Edition*, July 31–August 6, 1995. Available from Reprints, 1150 15th St. NW, Washington, DC 20071.
Congressional Digest	Issue on welfare reform, June/July 1995.
George Gilder	"End Welfare Reform As We Know It," *American Spectator*, June 1995.
Andrew Hacker	"The Crackdown on African-Americans," *Nation*, July 10, 1995.
Murray Hausknecht	"Institutionalizing Meanness," *Dissent*, Fall 1995.
Jobs & Capital	Special section on welfare reform, Winter 1995. Available from the Milken Institute for Jobs and Capital, 1250 Fourth St., 2nd Fl., Santa Monica, CA 90401-1353.
David Dyssegaard Kallick	"A Post-Liberal Approach to Welfare," *Social Policy*, Spring 1995.
Betty Reid Mandell	"Shredding the Safety Net," *New Politics*, Spring 1995.
David Moberg	"Reviving the Public Sector," *In These Times*, October 16–29, 1995.
Frances Fox Piven	"Poorhouse Politics," *Progressive*, February 1995.
E. Clay Shaw Jr.	"Welfare: 'This Fight Is Not Over,'" *Washington Post National Weekly Edition*, February 12–18, 1996.
Michael Tanner	"Ending Welfare As We Know It," *USA Today*, March 1995.
World & I	Special section on welfare, September 1995. Available from 3600 New York Ave. NE, Washington, DC 20002.
James Worsham	"Recasting Welfare," *Nation's Business*, November 1995.

2 CHAPTER

Does Welfare Encourage Dependency?

Chapter Preface

Tara Grandberry was raised on and off welfare. In 1995, Grandberry, 27, and her two young children themselves were receiving Aid to Families with Dependent Children (AFDC). In Grandberry's words:

> My daughter's father wasn't even around when she was born, and my husband left me for another woman when our son was five months old. Welfare hasn't helped me do better for myself. If I got a job paying $7.50 an hour, I'd lose my day care, most of my food stamps, and my rent would go up.

According to welfare critics, many poor single mothers spend years on welfare rolls, the result of out-of-wedlock births and a lack of desire to work. Furthermore, some commentators note, women such as Grandberry and single teenage mothers often succeed their parents—and even their grandparents—on the welfare rolls. In fact, a child raised on welfare is three times more likely than other children to receive welfare as an adult. Hence, observers commonly refer to the "cycle of dependency" to describe the current welfare system.

However, others contend that the prevalence of a "cycle of dependency" is an exaggeration. Children's Defense Fund president Marian Wright Edelman states, "Most welfare recipients are not on the rolls for long periods of time. Fifty percent of all people entering the welfare system leave within one year and 70 percent within two years. Only 15 percent stay for more than five years." According to Edelman and others, single mothers such as Grandberry stay on welfare longer than they want because they can support their families better on welfare than they could by working at the low-paying jobs available to them.

The authors in the following chapter debate whether welfare causes dependency and whether mothers can successfully make the transition from welfare to work.

"For the hard-core welfare recipient, the value of the full range of welfare benefits substantially exceeds the amount the recipient could earn in an entry-level job."

The High Value of Welfare Benefits Keeps the Poor on Welfare

Michael Tanner, Stephen Moore, and David Hartman

In the following viewpoint, Michael Tanner, Stephen Moore, and David Hartman maintain that the value of welfare benefits is more attractive to many long-term welfare recipients than are entry-level jobs. In several states, the authors contend, welfare programs pay recipients the equivalent of a $25,000-per-year job. Tanner is director of health and welfare studies and Moore is director of fiscal policy studies at the Cato Institute, a libertarian public policy research foundation in Washington, D.C. Hartman is CEO of Hartland Bank, N.A., in Austin, Texas.

As you read, consider the following questions:

1. What factor heightens the attractiveness of welfare, in the authors' opinion?
2. According to the authors, which benefit program is most often equated with welfare?
3. Why are welfare benefits higher in large cities, according to the authors?

Excerpted from Michael Tanner, Stephen Moore, and David Hartman, "The Work vs. Welfare Trade-Off," *Cato Policy Analysis*, September 19, 1995. Reprinted by permission from the Cato Institute.

The value of the full package of welfare benefits for a typical recipient in each of the 50 states and the District of Columbia exceeds the poverty level. Because welfare benefits are tax-free, their dollar value is often greater than the amount of take-home income a worker would have left after paying taxes on an equivalent pretax income.

• In 40 states welfare pays more than an $8.00 an hour job. In 17 states the welfare package is more generous than a $10.00 an hour job.

• In Hawaii, Alaska, Massachusetts, Connecticut, the District of Columbia, New York, and Rhode Island welfare pays more than a $12.00 an hour job—or two and a half times the minimum wage.

• In nine states welfare pays more than the average first-year salary for a teacher. In 29 states it pays more than the average starting salary for a secretary. And in the six most generous states it pays more than the entry-level salary for a computer programmer.

• Welfare benefits are especially generous in large cities. Welfare provides the equivalent of an hourly pretax wage of $14.75 in New York City, $12.45 in Philadelphia, $11.35 in Baltimore, and $10.90 in Detroit.

For the hard-core welfare recipient, the value of the full range of welfare benefits substantially exceeds the amount the recipient could earn in an entry-level job. As a result, recipients are likely to choose welfare over work, thus increasing long-term dependence.

A Rational Decision

As the debate over welfare reform heats up, one goal seems constant across the ideological spectrum. Nearly everyone agrees that a major goal of welfare reform should be to encourage recipients to leave the welfare rolls and enter the workforce. However, to date, there is no evidence that any of the policy prescriptions championed by either liberals (such as job training and child care) or conservatives (such as workfare) have been successful in achieving that goal. There appears to be a good reason for the failure.

Despite the stereotypes, there is no evidence that people receiving welfare are "lazy." Indeed, surveys of recipients consistently show that they express a desire to work. The choice of welfare over work is often a rational decision based on the economic incentives presented.

Most welfare recipients, particularly long-term recipients, lack the skills necessary to obtain the types of jobs that pay top or even average wages. The individuals who *do* leave welfare for work most often start employment in service or retail trade industries, generally as clerks, secretaries, cleaning persons, sales help, and waitresses. Although it would be nice to increase the wages of entry-level workers to the point where work paid better than welfare, government has no ability to do so. (Attempts to mandate wage increases, such as minimum wage legislation, result chiefly in increased unemployment.)

The Package of Benefits

Welfare advocacy groups and the media often portray welfare as a series of frugal programs that barely provide subsistence help to the needy. But that conclusion is based on the faulty assumption that welfare recipients receive primarily only one form of public assistance, Aid to Families with Dependent Children. But today at the federal, state, and local levels of government, there are dozens of welfare assistance programs in addition to AFDC. . . .

The attractiveness of welfare relative to work is heightened by the fact that welfare benefits are a nontaxable form of income.

Table 1 shows the total value of welfare relative to work by state. The full package of welfare benefits actually provides recipients with incomes above the poverty level in every state. There is a wide disparity among the states regarding the attractiveness of welfare. The value of the total package of benefits relative to a job providing the same after-tax income ranges from a high of $36,400 in Hawaii to a low of $11,500 in Mississippi. In eight jurisdictions—Hawaii, Alaska, Massachusetts, Connecticut, the District of Columbia, New York, New Jersey, and Rhode Island—welfare pays at least the equivalent of a $25,000 a year job.

The pretax value of welfare benefits substantially exceeds the amount a recipient could earn in an entry-level job in virtually every state. The numbers suggest that recipients of aid are likely to choose welfare over work, thus increasing their long-term dependence.

Although the evidence shows that, in the long term, an individual is better off in the labor force than on welfare, moving from welfare to work is likely to lead to at least a short-term decline in income and, for some, perhaps a permanent reduction of income. That may be why 68.6 percent of welfare recipients report that they are not actively seeking work. Other studies show that, as welfare benefits increase, women are more likely to leave the labor force and enroll in welfare programs instead.

Any welfare reform proposal must recognize that individuals are unlikely to move from welfare to work as long as welfare pays as well as or better than working. That suggests that the most promising welfare reforms are those that substantially cut back on the level of benefits.

Table 1. Wage Equivalent of Welfare, 1995

Rank	Jurisdiction	Pretax Wage Equivalent ($)	Hourly Wage ($)
1	Hawaii	36,400	17.50
2	Alaska	32,200	15.48
3	Massachusetts	30,500	14.66
4	Connecticut	29,600	14.23
5	District of Columbia	29,100	13.99
6	New York	27,300	13.13
7	New Jersey	26,500	12.74
8	Rhode Island	26,100	12.55
9	California	24,100	11.59
10	Virginia	23,100	11.11
11	Maryland	22,800	10.96
12	New Hampshire	22,800	10.96
13	Maine	21,600	10.38
14	Delaware	21,500	10.34
15	Colorado	20,900	10.05
16	Vermont	20,900	10.05
17	Minnesota	20,800	10.00
18	Washington	20,700	9.95
19	Nevada	20,200	9.71
20	Utah	19,900	9.57
21	Michigan	19,700	9.47
22	Pennsylvania	19,700	9.47
23	Illinois	19,400	9.33
24	Wisconsin	19,400	9.33
25	Oregon	19,200	9.23
26	Wyoming	19,100	9.18
27	Indiana	19,000	9.13
28	Iowa	19,000	9.13
29	New Mexico	18,600	8.94
30	Florida	18,200	8.75
31	Idaho	18,000	8.65
32	Oklahoma	17,700	8.51
33	Kansas	17,600	8.46
34	North Dakota	17,600	8.46
35	Georgia	17,400	8.37
36	Ohio	17,400	8.37
37	South Dakota	17,300	8.32
38	Louisiana	17,000	8.17
39	Kentucky	16,800	8.08
40	North Carolina	16,800	8.08
41	Montana	16,300	7.84
42	South Carolina	16,200	7.79
43	Nebraska	15,900	7.64
44	Texas	15,200	7.31
45	West Virginia	15,200	7.31
46	Missouri	14,900	7.16
47	Arizona	14,100	6.78
48	Tennessee	13,700	6.59
49	Arkansas	13,200	6.35
50	Alabama	13,000	6.25
51	Mississippi	11,500	5.53

Table 1 may actually understate the hourly wage equivalent because it is based on a 52-week (2,080-hour) work year and assumes no vacation.

Source: Michael Tanner, Stephen Moore, and David Hartman, *Cato Policy Analysis*, September 19, 1995.

In an attempt to determine whether there is an economic incentive to choose welfare over work, this viewpoint examines the welfare benefits that a typical household would receive in each state and the District of Columbia. The popular press often reports that welfare provides a barely subsistence level of assistance to low-income families and consumes only a small portion of the federal budget. That popular misconception results from examining only one federal welfare program, AFDC. The truth is that there are at least 77 major means-tested federal programs for the poor. State, county, and municipal governments operate additional welfare programs. Obviously, no one receives assistance from all of those programs, but most welfare recipients are eligible for a number of them. This viewpoint takes account of the programs from which welfare recipients are most likely to get benefits: AFDC, food stamps, Medicaid, public housing, nutrition assistance, and utility assistance. We calculate the combined value of benefits for a welfare recipient who fits a typical profile in each of the 50 states and the District of Columbia. We do not take into account special state and city low-income assistance programs that might be provided in addition to the major federal programs. Many of the smaller federal low-income assistance programs are also not accounted for. So actual benefit levels available to a welfare family may be somewhat higher. . . .

A Typical Household

In this analysis we use a profile of a typical welfare household consisting of a single mother over the age of 21 and two children, ages one and four. No paternity has been established for the children. The mother does not work and reports no outside income. Neither the mother nor either child is disabled. All are American citizens. That profile substantially conforms to the typical AFDC household.

We then compute the cash value of the total benefits package that the profiled household would be eligible to receive, using data for the most current year available. Those benefits are discussed in the following subsections.

Cash Benefits

AFDC. AFDC is the primary cash benefit program targeted to the poor and is the program most often considered "welfare." AFDC began in 1935 (it was then called Aid to Dependent Children) as part of the Social Security Act. The program provides cash payments to families with children whose father or mother is absent, incapacitated, deceased, or unemployed and to certain others in the households of those children. All 50 states, the District of Columbia, Puerto Rico, and Guam operate AFDC programs. American Samoa is eligible for the program but has chosen not to participate.

Each state determines its own benefit levels and (within certain federal restrictions) eligibility requirements. Funding comes from both the federal and the state governments, with the federal portion varying from a high of 80 percent to a low of 50 percent. On average, the federal government provides 55 percent of funding for AFDC.

In 1995 our profile household would be eligible for AFDC in all 50 states. The amount of AFDC benefits ranges from a high of $923 per month in Alaska to a low of $120 per month in Mississippi. The national average AFDC benefit is $399 per month.

Food and Medical Benefits

Food stamps. As the name implies, the food stamp program provides vouchers to low-income households for the purchase of food. Participating households are expected to spend 30 percent of their monthly cash income on food. The food stamp program contributes the difference between that amount and the amount judged to be sufficient to purchase an adequate diet. The food stamp program operates in all 50 states, the District of Columbia, Guam, Puerto Rico, and the Virgin Islands.

Eligibility standards and benefit levels are defined by the federal government, and, with the exceptions of Alaska, Hawaii, and the territories, they are uniform nationally. The maximum benefit level is derived from the U.S. Department of Agriculture's "Thrifty Food Plan," varied by household size, and adjusted annually for inflation.

Recipients of AFDC are automatically eligible for food stamps. Therefore, our profile household receives food stamps in every state. However, the value of food stamps received varies depending on the amount of the AFDC payment and the cost of food. Our household would receive the highest level of food stamps, $422, in Hawaii and the lowest, $192, in Connecticut. The high benefit level in Hawaii is largely due to the high price of food in that state. The low benefit in Connecticut is largely due to the extremely high AFDC benefits that Connecticut provides. The nationwide average is $278. . . .

Medicaid. The Medicaid program, Title XIX of the Social Security Act, was begun in 1965 and is the nation's primary program for providing health care for low-income people. Adults and children in low-income families make up nearly 75 percent of Medicaid recipients. . . .

As is AFDC, Medicaid is administered by the states within broad federal guidelines. Funding is divided between the federal and state governments, with the federal government's share ranging from 50 to 80 percent of the total. On average, the federal government funds about 57 percent of Medicaid costs.

States must provide Medicaid to all persons receiving cash assistance under AFDC. Thus, our profile household is eligible for Medicaid in all 50 states. . . .

Spending on Medicaid for our profile household ranges from a high of $6,086 in Alaska to a low of $1,171 in Arizona. . . .

Other Assistance Programs

Housing Assistance. Federal housing assistance comes in several forms. Three of those forms are: public housing, Housing Assistance Payments (better known as Section 8), and other rent subsidies. Section 8 payments can be further subdivided into three programs: the Section 8 Rental Voucher Program, the Section 8 Rental Certificate Program, and the Section 8 Moderate Rehabilitation Program.

A family is considered eligible for housing assistance if its household income falls below 50 percent of the median for a family of the same size in the same county. . . .

Utilities Assistance. There are several programs at both the federal and state level designed to help low-income households pay for heating oil, electricity, and other utilities.

In 1994 our profile household would have been eligible for utilities assistance, such as the federal Low Income Home Energy Assistance Program. While not all low-income households receive utilities assistance, participation levels in all states exceeded 50 percent. . . .

Special Supplemental Food Program. The Special Supplemental Food Program for Women, Infants, and Children (WIC) provides food assistance and nutritional screening for pregnant and postpartum women and their infants, as well as for low-income children up to the age of five. Beneficiaries receive vouchers for the purchase of specific food items (or occasionally actual foodstuffs). The actual food package depends on the ages of the children, whether the mother is pregnant, and whether a postpartum mother is nursing, but food packages generally include milk, cheese, eggs, infant formula, cereals, fruit, and vegetable juices.

The children in our profile household would have qualified for WIC in 1994. While not all eligible low-income households receive WIC benefits, approximately 56 percent of eligible families participate in the program nationwide. . . .

Estimating the Actual Value of Benefits

The second step in determining the actual value of the welfare benefits package was to compare the value of those benefits with the amount of pretax salary that a worker would have to earn to receive an equivalent after-tax income. . . .

The annual pretax salary [equivalent to the value of the welfare benefits package was then translated] into an hourly wage

81

rate. . . . In every state the equivalent hourly wage exceeded the minimum wage. Indeed, in 40 states welfare pays more than an $8.00 per hour job. In 17 states the welfare package is more generous than a $10.00 per hour job. In Hawaii, Alaska, Massachusetts, Connecticut, New York, Rhode Island, and the District of Columbia welfare pays more than a $12.00 per hour job, or nearly three times the minimum wage.

Two other comparisons are helpful in considering the real value of welfare benefits. The first is a comparison of the value of welfare benefits with the poverty level. In every state welfare benefits exceed the current poverty level of $11,817 for a family of three. In 21 states welfare benefits exceed 150 percent of the poverty level, and in Hawaii, Alaska, Connecticut, and Massachusetts the benefits package is more than 200 percent of the poverty level. Clearly, it is a myth that welfare has not kept pace with the official poverty level in America. . . .

The wage-equivalent value of welfare benefits is likely to be higher in large cities than in the states generally. There are two reasons for that. First, the value of public housing tends to be higher in urban areas. Second, 16 major cities have income or wage taxes that are in addition to the state income tax. City income taxes increase the financial attractiveness of welfare relative to work for residents. On the other hand, the cost of living and wages are often higher in urban areas than in outlying areas. . . .

The average welfare benefit in the 16 cities is comparable to a $10.00 an hour, 40-hour-a-week job. Hence, in cities, particularly those with income or wage taxes, especially high hurdles must be overcome to move long-term welfare dependents into work. . . .

The Key to Reform

It is, of course, possible to overgeneralize from the above statistics. Not every welfare recipient fits the profile, and many who do fit it do not receive all the benefits listed. Still, what is undeniable is that for many recipients—particularly long-term dependents—welfare pays substantially more than the type of entry-level job that a typical welfare recipient can expect to find. As long as that is true, recipients are likely to choose welfare over work. Hence, if Congress or state governments are serious about reducing hard-core welfare dependence and rewarding work, the most promising reform is to cut benefit levels substantially.

"It [is] nearly impossible for women to move off of welfare through work alone, without sufficient and stable supplemental income supports."

A Lack of Opportunities Keeps the Poor on Welfare

Chris Tilly and Randy Albelda

A variety of factors—including insufficient pay, a lack of good jobs, and the absence of health care and child care—combine to keep poor single mothers on welfare, Chris Tilly and Randy Albelda argue in the following viewpoint. Until employers provide adequate wages, benefits, and flexibility, they contend, welfare will remain the only viable option for many single mothers. Tilly teaches public policy at the University of Massachusetts in Lowell. Albelda teaches economics at the University of Massachusetts in Boston.

As you read, consider the following questions:

1. According to Tilly and Albelda, what is the "triple whammy" affecting single mothers?
2. How much does the average woman earn compared to her male counterpart, according to Tilly and Albelda?
3. What types of jobs are eliminated by raising the minimum wage, according to the authors?

Chris Tilly and Randy Albelda, "It's Not Working: Why Many Single Mothers Can't Work Their Way Out of Poverty," *Dollars & Sense*, November/December 1994. Reprinted by permission. *Dollars & Sense* is a progressive economics magazine published six times a year. First-year subscriptions cost $18.95 and may be ordered by writing to *Dollars & Sense*, One Summer St., Somerville, MA 02143.

but whether our government is or is not everyone has will.

Most current welfare reform proposals assume that all single mothers can simply work their way out of poverty—that it's a matter of will. President Bill Clinton's "two years and out" time limit on benefits before mandatory work, along with the renewed emphasis on job search and short-term training programs, arises from an increasingly common determination to have poor women lift themselves up by their bootstraps.

For many single mothers, this strategy cannot work. In the absence of universal child care, health care, and an abundance of good jobs, welfare plays a crucial role as a safety net. And even if the government were to offset the daunting demands of caring for children, provide health care, and brighten the limited opportunities at the bottom of the labor market, large numbers of single mothers would continue to require public assistance.

It's not for want of trying that single mothers have not been able to make ends meet. They work for pay about as many hours per year, on average, as other mothers: about 1,000 hours a year (a year-round, full-time job logs 2,000 hours). But less than full-time work for most women in this country just doesn't pay enough to feed mouths, make rent payments, and provide care for children while at work.

Not all single mothers are poor—but half of them are (compared to a 5% poverty rate for married couples). For poor single mothers, the labor market usually doesn't provide a ticket off of welfare or out of poverty. That's why AFDC (Aid to Families with Dependent Children, the program known as welfare) works like a revolving door for so many of them.

Heidi Hartmann and Roberta Spalter-Roth of the Institute for Women's Policy Research (IWPR) report that half of single mothers who spend any time on welfare during a two-year period also work for pay. But that work only generates about one-third of their families' incomes. In short, work is not enough; like other mothers, they "package" their income from three sources: work in the labor market, support from men or other family members, and government aid. "Mothers typically need at least two of those sources to survive," says Spalter-Roth.

The Triple Whammy

While all women, especially mothers, face barriers to employment with good wages and benefits, single mothers face a "triple whammy" that sharply limits what they can earn. Three factors—job discrimination against women, the time and money it takes to care for children, and the presence of only one adult—combine to make it nearly impossible for women to move off of welfare through work alone, without sufficient and stable supplemental income supports.

First, the average woman earns about two-thirds as much per

hour as her male counterpart. Women who need to rely on AFDC earn even less, since they often have lower skills, less work experience and more physical disabilities than other women. Between 1984 and 1988, IWPR researchers found, welfare mothers who worked for pay averaged a disastrous $4.18 per hour. Welfare mothers with jobs received employer-provided health benefits only one-quarter of the time. AFDC mothers are three times as likely as other women to work as maids, cashiers, nursing aides, child care workers, and waitresses—the lowest of the low-paid women's jobs.

©Simpson/Rothco. Used with permission.

Second, these families include kids. Like all mothers, single mothers have to deal with both greater demands on their time and larger financial demands—more "mouths to feed." A 1987 time-budget study found that the average time spent in household work for employed women with two or more children was 51 hours a week. Child care demands limit the time women can put into their jobs, and interrupt them with periodic crises, ranging from a sick child to a school's summer break. This takes its toll on both the amount and the quality of work many mothers can obtain. "There's a sad match between women's needs for a little flexibility and time, and the growth in contingent jobs, part-time jobs, jobs that don't last all year," comments Spalter-Roth. "That's the kind of jobs they're getting."

Finally, and unlike other mothers, single mothers have only one adult in the family to juggle child care and a job. Fewer adults means fewer opportunities for paid work. And while a single mother may receive child support from an absent father, she certainly cannot count on the consistent assistance—be it financial support or help with child care—that a resident father can provide.

A Bleak Labor Market

Suppose Clinton and company make good on their promise to give welfare mothers a quick shove into the labor market. What kind of prospects will they face there? Two-thirds of AFDC recipients hold no more than a high school diploma. The best way to tell how work requirements will work is to look at the women who already have the jobs that welfare recipients would be compelled to seek.

The news is not good. An unforgiving labor market, in recession and recovery alike, has hammered young, less-educated women, according to economists Jared Bernstein and Lawrence Mishel of the Economic Policy Institute, a Washington, D.C. think tank. Between 1979 and 1989, hourly wages plummeted for these women, falling most rapidly for African American women who didn't finish high school. This group's hourly wages, adjusted for inflation, fell 20% in that ten year period. Most young high-school-or-less women continued to lose during 1989–93. At the end of this losing streak, average hourly wages ranged from $5 an hour for younger high school dropouts to $8 an hour for older women with high school diplomas.

Unemployment rates in 1993 for most of these young women are stunning: 42% for black female high school dropouts aged 16–25, and 26% for their Latina counterparts.

But young women don't have a monopoly on labor market distress: workforce-wide hourly wages fell 14% between 1973 and 1993, after controlling for inflation. Given the collapse of wage rates, work simply is not enough to lift many families out of poverty. Two-thirds of all people living in poor families with children—15 million Americans—lived in families *with a worker* in 1991, report Isaac Shapiro and Robert Greenstein of the Center on Budget and Policy Priorities. And 5.5 million of these people in poverty had a family member who worked *year-round full-time*.

The problems of insufficient pay and time to raise children

86

that face single-mother families—and indeed many families—go far beyond the welfare system. So the solution must be much more comprehensive than simply reforming that system. What we need is a set of thorough changes in the relations among work, family, and income. Some of the Clinton administration's proposals actually fit into this larger package, but these positive elements are for the most part buried in get-tough posturing and wishful thinking. Here's what's needed:

• *Provide supports for low-wage workers.* The two most important supports are universal health coverage . . . and a universal child care plan. Two-thirds of welfare recipients leave the rolls within two years, but lack of health insurance and child care drive many of them back: over half of women who leave welfare to work come back to AFDC. A society that expects all able-bodied adults to work—regardless of the age of their children—should also be a society that socializes the costs of going to work, by offering programs to care for children of all ages.

• *Create jobs.* This item seems to have dropped off the national policy agenda. Deficit-phobia has hogtied any attempt at fiscal stimulus, and the Federal Reserve seems bent on stamping out growth in the name of preventing inflation. And yet Clinton and Congress could call for reform at the Fed, use government spending to boost job growth, and even invest in creating public service jobs.

• *Make work pay by changing taxes and government assistance.* Make it pay not only for women working their way off welfare, but for everybody at the low end of the labor market. Clinton's preferred tool for this has been the Earned Income Tax Credit (EITC)—which gives tax credits to low-wage workers with children (this tax provision now outspends AFDC). Although they get the EITC, women on welfare who work suffer a penalty that takes away nearly a dollar of the AFDC grant for every dollar earned. Making work pay would mean reducing or eliminating this penalty.

Improving Wages and Training

• *Make work pay by shoring up wages and benefits.* To ensure that the private sector does its part, raise the minimum wage. A full-time, year-round minimum wage job pays less than the poverty income threshold for a family of one. Conservatives and the small business lobby will trot out the bogeyman of job destruction, but studies on the 1991 minimum wage increase showed a zero or even positive effect on employment. Hiking the minimum wage does eliminate lousy jobs, but the greater purchasing power created by a higher wage floor generates roughly the same number of *better* jobs. In addition, mandate benefit parity for part-time, temporary, and subcontracted workers. This would close a loophole that a growing number of employers use to dodge fringe benefits.

• *Make a serious commitment to life-long education and training.* Education and training do help welfare recipients and other disadvantaged workers. But significant impacts depend on longer-term, intensive—and expensive—programs. We also need to expand training to a broader constituency, since training targeted only to the worst-off workers helps neither these workers, who get stigmatized in the eyes of employers, nor the remainder of the workforce, who get excluded. In Sweden, half the workforce takes some time off work for education in any given year.

Flexibility and Filling Gaps

• *Build flexibility into work.* "Increasingly," says Spalter-Roth, "all men and all women are workers *and* nurturers." Some unions have begun to bargain for the ability to move between full-time and part-time work, but in most workplaces changing hours means quitting a job and finding a new one. And though employees now have the right to unpaid family or medical leave, many can't afford to take time off. *Paid* leave would, of course, solve this problem. Failing that, temporary disability insurance (TDI) that is extended beyond disability situations to those facing a wide range of family needs could help. Five states (California, New York, New Jersey, Rhode Island, and Hawaii) currently run TDI systems funded by payroll taxes.

• *Mend the safety net, for times when earnings aren't enough.* Unemployment insurance has important gaps: low-wage earners receive even lower unemployment benefits, the long-term unemployed get cut off, new labor market entrants and re-entrants have no access to benefits, and in many states people seeking part-time work cannot collect. Closing these gaps would help welfare "packagers," as well as others at the low end of the labor market, to make ends meet. But even with all of these policies in place, there will be times when single mothers will either choose or be compelled to set aside paid work, sometimes for extended periods, to care for their families. For the foreseeable future, we still need Aid to Families with Dependent Children as a backstop. But at its current level, AFDC rarely acts as a safety net: Hartmann and Spalter-Roth found that AFDC recipients without significant earnings received incomes worth only two-thirds of the poverty line on average.

So welcome to reality. Most single mothers *cannot* work their way out of poverty—definitely not without supplemental support. There are many possible policy steps that could be taken to help them and other low-wage workers get the most out of an inhospitable labor market. But ultimately, old-fashioned welfare must remain part of the formula.

"Research findings on serving teen parents have demonstrated that large-scale mandatory programs for teen parents can produce results."

Government Programs Help Teen Mothers Get Off Welfare

Pat Rowe

Pat Rowe is the assistant editor of *Children Today,* a quarterly magazine published by the federal Administration for Children and Families in Washington, D.C. In the following viewpoint, Rowe argues that state job and educational programs targeting teen mothers can help them make the transition from welfare to self-sufficiency. She contends that such programs have produced positive results in terms of keeping teen mothers in school and employed.

As you read, consider the following questions:

1. How does alternative schooling differ from regular schooling, according to Rowe?
2. According to the author, what types of services do community agencies provide?
3. Which group of teenagers does Ohio's Learning, Earning and Parenting Program target, according to Rowe?

Pat Rowe, "ACF Supports Efforts to Serve Teen Parents," *Children Today*, vol. 23, no. 2, 1994.

Through the Job Opportunities and Basic Skills Training (JOBS) Program, the Administration for Children and Families (ACF) is making teen parents a top priority in order to help them achieve self-sufficiency as quickly as possible. Such efforts will further the vision of the Administration's welfare reform initiative, which focuses on this population.

ACF Assistant Secretary Mary Jo Bane points out, "While we recognize that we must do everything we can to prevent young people from going on welfare in the first place, our system needs to do a better job in fulfilling the mandate of the JOBS Program to more effectively serve teen parents. If we are to be successful in making welfare a transitional support program, we must continue to focus on the teen parent population. We must work together with the States to see how to implement requirements for teen parents more effectively."

To support States in their efforts to serve teens, ACF's Office of Family Assistance (OFA), which administers the JOBS program, issued an Information Memorandum [IM] in June 1994 entitled, "Serving Teen Parents in JOBS." This paper shares information about current research findings and features State JOBS programs that have taken positive steps toward implementing effective programs for teenage parents.

Teen Parents' Needs

It examines the characteristics and needs of teen parents; identifies alternative program strategies that may be considered; presents findings from research related to education, training, and employment programs for teen parents; and provides summaries of current State programs with contact information.

The Family Support Act of 1988 (the Act) recognized that teen parents and the families they head are at high risk of long-term welfare dependency. A number of specific provisions were included in the Act to ensure that State JOBS programs addressed the educational needs of these young parents. In addition, all State JOBS programs are expected to serve the majority of teen parents who are required to participate in educational activities.

States have significant latitude to design their JOBS programs to address the specific needs or circumstances of their teenage parent population in the context of the local environment. The programs featured in the Information Memorandum, "Serving Teen Parents in JOBS," present examples of a variety of administrative and service delivery approaches that can be used to meet the objectives of the Act. The following discussion contains highlights from the Information Memorandum.

According to OFA, research findings on serving teen parents have demonstrated that large-scale mandatory programs for teen parents can produce results. The Teen Parent Demonstration

Program, which operated in Camden and Newark, New Jersey, and Chicago, Illinois, showed that teen mothers on AFDC [Aid to Families with Dependent Children] who were part of a mandatory training and supportive services program achieved and maintained significantly higher rates of school attendance and employment. Ohio's Learning, Earning and Parenting (LEAP) demonstration is also showing encouraging interim results in terms of significantly increasing school retention and encouraging teens to return to school or adult education.

Identification of eligible teens is a precursor to serving them in JOBS and often presents a challenge for States since dependent teen parents are difficult to identify. They are often "buried" in cases where someone else, usually the teen's mother, is the case head.

Financial Incentives

Given the importance of education to help AFDC teens achieve self-sufficiency, many demonstration programs are testing the impact of financial incentives (both bonuses and sanctions) to keep teens, including JOBS teen parents, in school. Demonstrations require waivers from regular JOBS or AFDC program requirements.

Research results from Ohio's LEAP Program demonstration, which uses a combination of bonuses and sanctions, and the Teen Parent Demonstration Program in Illinois and New Jersey (1987-1991), which used only sanctions, strongly support the use of financial incentives to encourage teens to attend school. A number of other States are testing the use of financial incentives to keep teens in school.

Enriched Educational Services

Based on research, GAO's [General Accounting Office] analysis and State/local experience, the provision of enriched services—including life skills training, parenting classes or alternative schooling—is an important factor in helping teen parents complete their education.

Some public school systems have made conscious efforts to improve their services to pregnant and parenting teens, hoping to make school more relevant to their needs and more "do-able" in terms of their responsibilities. Some systems work with JOBS participants through extra or special services in their regular schools and programs. In Ohio, the Graduation, Reality and Dual Role Skills (GRADS) program was very important to the success of LEAP. Available in many school districts, GRADS has provided parenting skills, life skills and employment-related classes to pregnant and parenting teens, including LEAP participants.

Arizona, Ohio and Illinois offer both traditional and alternative

91

schooling to teen parents. Alternative school programs are usually designed to address the special needs of "non-traditional" students such as teen parents. These needs are not customarily addressed by the regular public school system. Such programs generally offer special courses, intensive case management, flexible scheduling and programming, lower student-staff ratios, and non-traditional teaching methods. Frequently, they provide a wide range of such support services as child care, transportation, and courses or support sessions in life skills.

Strong Case Management

Even the more successful state and local teen parent programs vary in case management methodology, as well as in caseload size and responsibilities of the case manager. This makes it difficult to recommend a single case management strategy or optimal caseload size for serving teen parents. However, all of the demonstration and ongoing teen parent programs described in OFA's IM have a strong commitment to case management as demonstrated by continued follow-up and monitoring, especially to ensure school attendance.

In some programs, such as Arizona, Arkansas, Alaska, Ohio, and Rhode Island, the case management function is shared by JOBS staff and on-site school staff. Case managers in the larger programs like Illinois and Ohio were able to work with relatively large caseloads (averaging about 80 to well over 100).

These States suggest that in assigning caseloads, attention needs to be paid to the portion of assigned cases that require ongoing case management study. Case management training is needed in such areas as adolescent development, health and pregnancy prevention and counseling principles. Caseloads also contain cases needing little ongoing case management, such as inactive cases (individuals who have been sanctioned or deferred) and stable cases (clients who are well established in ongoing training or education programs).

Community Agencies and Dedicated Staff

While many AFDC teen parents need little or no outside assistance to stay in and complete high school, others have serious and interrelated problems. Where some needs can be dealt with directly by case workers as an ongoing part of case management, programs have often found it best to link teen parents with community agencies that specialize in dealing with specific problems.

Community agencies provide resources for problems beyond the bounds of the JOBS or teen parent program but which, nevertheless, impact on the teen parent's ability to utilize that program. Needs like housing, child support, food and clothing, preventive health services or medical equipment are often best handled by referrals to agencies that specialize in those areas.

Substantial staff training and skilled supervision are needed to help case managers work effectively with the more difficult cases. Some teen parents bring a range of complex, interconnected problems. Often they live in dangerous neighborhoods and have relatively few role models in their communities to guide them toward social and economic independence. They often lack the motivation and self-esteem to continue their education or training. It takes a dedicated, committed staff to work with and help these teen parents and their families.

Toward Self-Sufficiency

The Teenage Parent Welfare Demonstration program showed that it is possible to achieve high rates of participation in activities oriented toward self-sufficiency—such as education or job training—so long as program staff members are committed to work with the young mothers to remove the barriers they face and are willing to use financial sanctions constructively to underscore the responsibilities of parenthood. . . .

Three programs [in Chicago and New Jersey] succeeded in enrolling nearly 90% of the teenage mothers they targeted. However, this high enrollment rate rested on the emphasis given to mandatory participation requirements and on the efforts of case managers to coax, pressure, and cajole troubled and uncooperative teenage parents into joining the program. Only one-third of these young mothers responded to routine notices about the program participation requirements, but follow-up communications and threats of grant reduction increased the percentage joining the program by an additional 50 points.

J. Lawrence Aber, Jeane Brooks-Gunn, and Rebecca A. Maynard, *The Future of Children*, Summer/Fall 1995.

LEAP (Ohio) and Illinois staff report that it is critical to keep trying to work with teens who are resistant, because they often change their minds. Many initially resistant teens were coaxed into the programs and successfully completed their high school educations.

The large-scale programs, Ohio's LEAP and Teen Parent Demonstration, have tied financial incentives to program participation. This has reinforced the obligation of young mothers to take charge of their lives and work toward self-sufficiency, as well as the responsibility of the program to help them move in this direction. The impact of these demonstrations supports the use of financial incentives to increase rates of school attendance for this population.

Demonstration Programs

• *The Teen Parent Demonstration.* Operated in New Jersey and Illinois, the Teen Parent Demonstration Program showed that teen mothers on AFDC achieved and sustained significantly higher rates of school attendance and employment when they were part of a mandatory training and support services program. The random assignment study, conducted by Mathematica Policy Research, Inc. under contract to the U.S. Department of Health and Human Services, tracked almost 6,000 young, first-time mothers in Camden and Newark, New Jersey, and Chicago, Illinois, from late 1987 to mid-1991.

• *Learning, Earning and Parenting (LEAP) Program.* Ohio's LEAP program is a statewide initiative requiring all pregnant and parenting teenage welfare recipients without a high school diploma or its equivalent to attend school regularly. LEAP is being implemented by the Ohio Department of Human Services (DHS), in cooperation with the public school systems and adult education entities in Ohio.

After three years of implementation, LEAP is showing encouraging interim results: LEAP appears to have prevented some in-school teen parents from dropping out and brought some teen parent dropouts back to school. School enrollment for LEAP teens in school when the program began was 10% higher than for control group teens; and LEAP participants who had dropped out of school were more likely to return to high school or enter adult education (13%) than were out of school teens in the control group.

LEAP found a relationship between the amount of time since the teens dropped out of school and the institution to which they returned. Recent drop-outs—those who had left school within a year before entry into LEAP—usually returned to high school. Those who had dropped out more than a year before were more likely to enter adult education programs.

A Variety of Services

• *New Chance.* New Chance is a research demonstration designed to identify effective models to help teen mothers and their children break the cycle of dependency. It is being conducted in 16 sites in 10 States: Chula Vista, California; Inglewood, California; San Jose, California; Denver, Colorado; Jacksonville, Florida; Chicago Heights, Illinois; Lexington, Kentucky; Detroit, Michigan; Minneapolis, Minnesota; Bronx, N.Y.; New York City (Harlem), N.Y.; Portland, Oregon; Salem, Oregon; Allentown, Pennsylvania; Philadelphia, Pennsylvania; and Pittsburgh, Pennsylvania.

94

New Chance is a voluntary program with a multigenerational focus. It targets welfare recipients 16–22 years old who lack a high school diploma or GED [Graduate Equivalency Degree], who first gave birth at age 19 or younger and are not pregnant at program entry. It provides adult basic education, GED, employability development, career exploration, work experience/internships, skills training and decision-making/life management training for the teen parents as well as health and personal development services such as parenting training and health education.

Developmental child care (provided on-site, where possible) and health screenings are available. Services are integrated and intensive. Case managers work intensively with the teens during program enrollment as well as after the teens secure employment. While the program model is consistent, the operational organization of New Chance sites is different; they are operated by community-based organizations, schools, community colleges, or government agencies.

• *ACF Teen Parent "Enhanced" Services Grants.* In September 1992, ACF awarded demonstration grants to 15 JOBS programs in 14 States (Alaska, Colorado, Georgia, Illinois, Kansas, Kentucky, Maryland, Massachusetts, Michigan, Minnesota, Montana, Oregon, Tennessee, and Wisconsin) to support enhancements to existing programs that provide comprehensive services to AFDC teen parents and to their children.

"Voluntary education and job-training programs may simply be unable to help enough unwed mothers escape long-term dependency."

Government Programs Do Not Help Teen Mothers Get Off Welfare

Douglas J. Besharov and Karen N. Gardiner

In the following viewpoint, Douglas J. Besharov and Karen N. Gardiner contend that three large-scale education and job-training programs have failed to end welfare dependency among teen mothers. These programs, Besharov and Gardiner argue, did not make teen participants more self-sufficient than members of corresponding control groups who did not participate in the programs. Besharov is a resident scholar and Gardiner is a research associate at the American Enterprise Institute, a conservative think tank in Washington, D.C.

As you read, consider the following questions:

1. What percentage of out-of-wedlock births are to teen mothers, according to Besharov and Gardiner?
2. What do Besharov and Gardiner criticize about New Chance's focus on the Graduate Equivalency Degree?
3. In the authors' opinion, what factor should have given the New Chance and Comprehensive Child Development projects an advantage?

Douglas J. Besharov and Karen N. Gardiner, "Paternalism and Welfare Reform." Reprinted, with permission, from the *Public Interest*, Winter 1996; ©1996, National Affairs, Inc.

Unwed parenthood among teenagers is a particularly serious problem. Between 1960 and 1993, the proportion of out-of-wedlock births among teenagers rose from 15 percent to 71 percent, with the absolute number of out-of-wedlock births rising from 89,000 to 369,000.

Teen mothers are now responsible for about 30 percent of all out-of-wedlock births, but even this understates the impact of unwed teen parenthood on the nation's illegitimacy problem. Sixty percent of all out-of-wedlock births involve mothers who had their first babies as teenagers.

Because so many unwed teen mothers have dropped out of school and have poor earnings prospects in general, they are even more likely to become long-term welfare recipients. Families begun by teenagers (married or unmarried) account for the majority of welfare expenditures in this country. According to Kristin Moore, executive director of Child Trends, Inc., 59 percent of women currently receiving Aid to Families with Dependent Children (AFDC) were 19 years old or younger when they had their first child. . . .

There should be no denying that the inability of most unwed mothers to earn as much as their welfare package is a major reason why they go on welfare—and stay there for so long. (A common route off welfare is marriage, but that is a subject for another article.) Hence, since the 1960s, most attempts to reduce welfare dependency have focused on raising the earnings capacity of young mothers through a combination of educational and job-training efforts. Given the faith Americans have in education as the great social equalizer, this emphasis has been entirely understandable. However, the evaluations of three major demonstration projects serve as an unambiguous warning that a new approach is needed.

Three Demonstration Projects

Beginning in the late 1980s, three large-scale demonstration projects designed to reduce welfare dependency were launched. Although the projects had somewhat different approaches, they all sought to foster self-sufficiency through a roughly similar combination of education, training, various health-related services, counseling, and, in two of the three, family planning.

• New Chance tried to avert long-term welfare recipiency by enhancing the "human capital" of young, welfare-dependent mothers. Designed and evaluated by Manpower Demonstration Research Corporation (MDRC), the program targeted those at especially high risk of long-term dependency: young welfare recipients (ages 16 to 22) who had their first child as a teenager and were also high-school dropouts. Its two-stage program attempted to remedy the mothers' severe educational deficits—

primarily through the provision of a Graduate Equivalency Degree (GED) and building specific job-related skills.

• The Teen Parent Demonstration attempted to use education and training services to increase the earnings potential of teen mothers before patterns of dependency took root. Evaluated by Mathematica Policy Research, the program required all first-time teen mothers in Camden and Newark, New Jersey, and the south side of Chicago, Illinois, to enroll when they first applied for welfare. The program enforced its mandate by punishing a mother's truancy through a reduction in her welfare grant.

• The Comprehensive Child Development Program (CCDP), which is still operating, seeks to break patterns of intergenerational poverty by providing an enriched developmental experience for children and educational services to their parents. A planned five-year intervention is designed to enhance the intellectual, social, and physical development of children from age one until they enter school. Although not a requirement for participation, the majority of families are headed by single parents. The program, evaluated by Abt Associates, also provides classes on parenting, reading, and basic skills (including GED preparation), as well as other activities to promote self-sufficiency. . . .

Teen Mothers' Disadvantages

All three projects served populations predominantly comprised of teen mothers and those who had been teens when they first gave birth. The average age at first birth was 17 for New Chance and Teen Parent Demonstration clients, while half of the CCDP clients were in their teens when they first gave birth. As the project evaluators soon found, this is an extremely disadvantaged—and difficult to reach—population. Over 60 percent of Teen Parent Demonstration and New Chance clients grew up in families that had received AFDC at some point in the past. If anything, early parenthood worsened their financial situations. All Teen Parent Demonstration clients, of course, were on welfare, as were 95 percent of those in New Chance. The average annual income for CCDP families was $5,000.

The mothers also suffered from substantial educational deficiencies. Although most were in their late teens or early twenties, few had high-school diplomas or GEDs. Many of those still in school (in the Teen Parent Demonstration) were behind by a grade. In New Chance and the Teen Parent Demonstration, the average mother was reading at the eighth-grade level. Their connections to the labor market were tenuous at best. Almost two-thirds of the New Chance participants had not worked in the year prior to enrollment, and 60 percent had never held a job for more than six months. Only half of Teen Parent Demonstration mothers had ever had a job. These young mothers also

98

had a variety of emotional or personal problems. About half of New Chance clients and about 40 percent of those in CCDP were diagnosed as suffering clinical depression. The mothers also reported problems with drinking and drug abuse. Many were physically abused by boyfriends.

Disappointing Results

Besides the intensity of the intervention, what set these three demonstrations apart from past efforts is that they were rigorously evaluated using random assignment to treatment and control groups. Random-assignment evaluations are especially important in this area because, at first glance, projects like these often look successful. For example, one demonstration site announced that it was successful because half of its clients had left welfare, and their earnings and rate of employment had both doubled. These results sound impressive, but the relevant policy question is: What would have happened in the absence of the project? This is called the "counterfactual," and it is the essence of judging the worth of a particular intervention.

Little Improvement for Young Mothers

Even richly funded demonstration programs have found it exceedingly difficult to improve the ability of [young] mothers to care for their children, let alone to become economically self-sufficient.

A six-county evaluation of California's [job training] program, for example, found that over two years, average earnings for single parents increased by 20 percent—three or four times the usual experience for such programs. Still, total earnings reached only $4,620. The county with the greatest improvement, Riverside, was able to increase earnings by $2,099, although average total earnings over two years were still less than $6,000. The welfare rolls declined by only 5 percent in Riverside, and by a statistically insignificant amount across all of the other counties.

Douglas J. Besharov, *Washington Post National Weekly Edition*, December 20–26, 1993.

Unfortunately, despite the effort expended, none of these demonstrations came anywhere near achieving its goals. After the intervention, the families in the control groups (which received no special services, but often did receive services outside of the demonstrations) were doing about as well, and sometimes better, than those in the demonstrations. In other words, the evaluations were unable to document any substantial differences in the lives of the families served. Here is a sample of their disappointing findings.

All three evaluations were unanimous: Participants were as likely to remain on welfare as those in the control groups. Robert Granger, senior vice president of MDRC, summed up the interim evaluation of New Chance: "This program at this particular point has not made people better off economically." At the end of 18 months, 82 percent of New Chance clients were on welfare compared to 81 percent of the control group. The Teen Parent Demonstration mothers did not fare any better. After two years, 71 percent were receiving AFDC, only slightly fewer than the control group (72.5 percent). CCDP participants were actually 5 percent more likely to have received welfare in the past year than were those in the control group (66 percent versus 63 percent).

Earnings and Work

Only the Teen Parent Demonstration program saw any gains in employment. Its mothers were 12 percent more likely to be employed sometime during the two years after the program began (48 percent of the treatment group versus 43 percent of the control group) and, as a result, averaged $23 per month more in income. In most cases, however, employment did not permanently end their welfare dependency. Nearly one in three of those who left AFDC for work returned within six months, 44 percent within a year, and 65 percent within three years.

The other programs did not show even this small gain. Fewer New Chance clients were employed during the evaluation period than controls (43 percent versus 45 percent), in part because they were in classes during some of the period. Those who did work tended to work for a short time, usually less than three months. Given the lower level of work, New Chance clients had earned 25 percent less than the control group at the time of the evaluation ($1,366 versus $1,708 a year). Only 29 percent of the CCDP mothers were working at the time of the two-year evaluation, the same proportion as the control group; there was no difference in the number of hours worked per week, the wages earned per week, or the number of months spent working.

Education and Training

All three demonstrations were relatively successful in enrolling mothers in education programs. Teen Parent Demonstration mothers were over 40 percent more likely to be in school (41 percent versus 29 percent), and about one-third of the CCDP clients were working towards a degree, 78 percent more than the control group.

About three-quarters more New Chance participants received their GED than their control-group counterparts (37 percent versus 21 percent). But the mothers' receiving a GED did not seem to raise their employability—or functional literacy. The average reading level of the New Chance mothers remained unchanged (eighth grade) and was identical to that of the control group. This finding echoes those from evaluations of other programs with similar goals, including the Department of Education's Even Start program. Jean Layzer, senior associate at Abt Associates, concluded that, rather than honing reading, writing, and math skills, GED classes tended to focus on test-taking: "What people did was memorize what they needed to know for the GED. They think that their goal is the GED because they think it will get them a job. But it won't—it won't give them the skills to read an ad in the newspaper."

In this light, it is especially troubling that, while increasing the number of GED recipients, New Chance seems to have reduced the number of young mothers who actually finished high school (6 percent versus 9 percent). According to one evaluator, the projects may have legitimated a young mother's opting for a GED rather than returning to high school.

Subsequent Births

Although the young mothers in New Chance and the Teen Parent Demonstration said they wanted to delay or forgo future childbearing, the majority experienced a repeat pregnancy within the evaluation period, and most opted to give birth. Mothers in one project spent only 1.5 hours on family planning, while they spent 54 hours in another, with no discernible difference in impact.

All New Chance sites offered family-planning classes and life-skills courses that sought to empower women to take control of their fertility. Many also dispensed contraceptives. In the Teen Parent Demonstration, the family-planning workshop was mandatory. Despite these efforts, over 7 percent more New Chance mothers experienced a pregnancy (57 percent versus 53 percent). One-fourth of both Teen Parent Demonstration clients and the control group experienced a pregnancy within one year; half of each group did so by the two-year follow-up. Two-thirds of all pregnancies resulted in births. Although it was hoped that the CCDP intervention would reduce subsequent births, this was not an explicit goal of the demonstration; nor was family planning a core service provided by the sites. But, again, there was no real difference between experimental and control groups: 30 percent of mothers in both had had another birth by the two-year follow-up. . . .

All in all, it's a sad story. But what is most discouraging about these results is that the projects, particularly New Chance and CCDP, enjoyed high levels of funding, yet still seemed unable to

COSUMNES RIVER COLLEGE
LEARNING RESOURCE CENTER

improve the lives of disadvantaged families. There are several explanations for their poor performance: Many of the project sites had no prior experience providing such a complex set of services; some were poorly managed; and almost all were plagued with the problems that typically characterize demonstration projects, such as slow start-ups, inexperienced personnel, and high staff turnover. In addition, the projects often chose the wrong objectives and tactics. For example, most focused on helping the mothers obtain GEDs, even in the face of accumulating evidence that the GED does not increase employability. As for the two programs that attempted to reduce subsequent births, program staff tried to walk a fine line between promoting the postponement of births and not devaluing the women's role as mothers. Their sessions on family planning seemed to have emphasized that the mothers should decide whether or not to have additional children—rather than that they should avoid having another child until they are self-sufficient.

But even such major weaknesses do not explain the dearth of positive impacts across so many goals—and so many sites. One would expect some signs of improvement in the treatment group if the projects had at least been on the right track. Hence, one is impelled to another explanation: The underlying strategy may be wrong. Voluntary education and job-training programs may simply be unable to help enough unwed mothers escape long-term dependency.

Periodical Bibliography

The following articles have been selected to supplement the diverse views presented in this chapter. Addresses are provided for periodicals not indexed in the *Readers' Guide to Periodical Literature*, the *Alternative Press Index*, or the *Social Sciences Index*.

Douglas J. Besharov	"On the Reform of Welfare with Continued Dependency," *Jobs & Capital*, Winter 1995. Available from Milken Institute for Jobs and Capital, 1250 Fourth St., 2nd Fl., Santa Monica, CA 90401-1353.
George Miller and James M. Talent	"Should Congress Halt Welfare Benefits for Unwed Teenage Mothers?" *American Legion Magazine*, May 1995. Available from PO Box 1055, Indianapolis, IN 46206.
Kristin A. Moore	"Welfare Bill Won't Stop Teenage Pregnancy," *Christian Science Monitor*, December 18, 1995. Available from 1 Norway St., Boston, MA 02115.
Bob Packwood	"Welfare Must Encourage Self-Reliance," *Insight*, April 17, 1995. Available from 3600 New York Ave. NE, Washington, DC 20002.
Mark R. Rank and Li-Chen Cheng	"Welfare Use Across Generations: How Important Are the Ties That Bind?" *Journal of Marriage and the Family*, August 1995. Available from 3989 Central Ave. NE, Suite 550, Minneapolis, MN 55421-3921.
Betsy Reed	"Welfare Programs That Work, and Those That Win," *Dollars & Sense*, November/December 1994.
Louis Sahagun	"Teen-Age Mothers at Eye of Welfare Storm," *Los Angeles Times*, February 14, 1995. Available from Reprints, Times Mirror Square, Los Angeles, CA 90053.
Society	"Reducing Welfare Dependency," May/June 1995.
Tracy Thompson	"Nature's Laws vs. Economic Theory," *Washington Post National Weekly Edition*, June 12–18, 1995. Available from Reprints, 1150 15th St. NW, Washington, DC 20071.
Time	"The Vicious Cycle," June 20, 1994.
Ann Scott Tyson	"Federal Program Helping Teenage Moms," *Christian Science Monitor*, December 12, 1994.

Is Abuse of the Welfare System a Serious Problem?

WELFARE

Chapter Preface

Welfare reformers on the left and the right believe that the costs of the system could be significantly reduced if abuse and fraud were eliminated. Many critics contend that men who father unwanted children and neglect to support them are the worst abusers of the welfare system. Katha Pollitt, an associate editor of *Nation*, estimates that 50 percent of welfare mothers are on the rolls due to the failure of fathers to pay adequate child support. Citing figures from the U.S. Department of Health and Human Services, she asserts that billions of dollars of court-ordered child support goes uncollected every year. Pollitt and other critics maintain that the welfare burden could be lightened if the fathers of impoverished children were forced to pay their fair share in child support.

Other commentators, however, do not agree that increased efforts to collect money from fathers will alleviate the costs of the welfare system. They contend that many of the fathers who are delinquent in paying support cannot afford to pay because they are unemployed or impoverished themselves. Laurie Casey, a senior analyst with the Children's Rights Council, estimates that 90 percent of fathers who are able to pay do so without being coerced by courts or the government. She argues that punitive efforts to force fathers to pay will cost more money to administer than they will raise for needy children.

The viewpoints in the following chapter examine whether eliminating purported fraud and abuse of the welfare system is an effective way of saving money and reducing poverty.

"Half [of aid recipients] will remain on welfare for more than ten years, and many are on it essentially for life."

Welfare Is a Way of Life for Some Women

Rachel Wildavsky and Daniel R. Levine

Some proponents of welfare reform argue that recipients become dependent on the system and over time find it increasingly difficult to leave. In the following viewpoint, Rachel Wildavsky and Daniel R. Levine describe the lives of three welfare mothers, all of whom have had additional children while on welfare. Wildavsky and Levine contend that these portraits demonstrate the damage the cycle of welfare dependency does to the lives of recipients and their children. Wildavsky is a senior staff editor and Levine is an associate editor for *Reader's Digest*.

As you read, consider the following questions:

1. What types of benefits are included in Marie A.'s welfare, according to Wildavsky and Levine?
2. In Cindy K.'s words, quoted by the authors, why did she want to have her first child?
3. Why doesn't Denise B. work even though she would like to, according to the authors?

Today, the United States spends well over $300 billion per year on welfare—up more than $100 billion from just ten years ago. Nearly five million households receive benefits under the main federally funded program, Aid to Families with Dependent Children (AFDC).

For some recipients government aid is a quick bridge over troubled times. But half will remain on welfare for more than ten years, and many are on it essentially for life. The fate of their children is also bleak: a child raised on welfare is three times more likely than other children to receive aid as an adult.

Today, as welfare reform is being debated, we need to know more about the people behind the statistics. For several months, two Reader's Digest editors traveled America, talking with people on welfare. Here are the actual life stories of three such welfare mothers. Names have been changed to protect the privacy of the children.

Marie A.

Marie A. of Germantown, Md., is a short, plump woman with a sharp temper. She says she "hates" welfare, insisting that she is different from her mother, who "could have worked," but was on the dole for more than 30 years. Now 43, Marie has had nine children by five different fathers. She has been arrested several times for shoplifting and has spent time in jail. Her welfare includes rent-free housing, food-stamp benefits, Medicaid and—when any of her minor children are living with her—tax-free cash grants through the AFDC program.

Marie's mother had five children by four different men, and when Marie was growing up in the Washington, D.C., area, all of the children were "bounced around a lot." Marie stopped attending school in the seventh grade and became pregnant at 15. She moved in with her 17-year-old boyfriend and hoped to marry him. But her boyfriend's interest in her flagged, and she soon learned his home was a factory for the drugs in which he dealt. She moved out.

In the next nine years Marie married twice and bore six more children by three different fathers. Both of her husbands were in the armed services, and she claims both beat her; laughingly, she recalls shooting at each in retaliation.

Sporadically throughout this period, Marie worked, usually as a waitress at "good-paying jobs." But in 1982 she went on welfare and moved into subsidized housing. "I've been on public assistance ever since," she says.

In 1985 she met Sam, 20, as he parked cars at a lot in Washington. The day they met, she told him, "I'm taking you home." He has been her boyfriend ever since.

Home was a comfortable, three-bedroom townhouse complete with dining room, den, laundry room, dishwasher and microwave on a neat, peaceful block in Woodbridge, Va. It was rent-free, courtesy of a federal program that provides subsidized housing to welfare families in non-welfare neighborhoods.

Marie had two children by Sam. She says she didn't want either child and over the years has had "four or five abortions." With the last child's birth, Marie reached her maximum allowable AFDC grant, $518 per month. At that point she had herself surgically sterilized. Lesser forms of birth control "don't seem to work on me," she says.

Marie lived in Woodbridge ten years. In the end, though, repeated complaints by neighbors forced her out. The neighbors described, among other things, violence among members of the household and threats toward others. Marie admits she "knocked [one neighbor] on her butt," but says the neighbors "had it in for me."

In Marie's last two years in Woodbridge, police officers were called to her home 72 times. By the time the family left, in August 1994, rubbish littered their yard, and the inside of their house was damaged and filmy with grime.

Despite that, Marie obtained another rent-free home, this time in a bucolic neighborhood in Germantown. It is an $87,000 townhouse with four bedrooms, 2½ baths, a dining room and an enclosed patio. Boyfriend Sam says he lives with his mother in Washington, but he spends most of his time at the Germantown home.

Marie has furnished the townhouse with, among other things, a king-sized waterbed, three color TVs—at least one with cable—and a comprehensive sound and video system, recently upgraded by Sam at, she boasts, a cost of $2500.

Yet just one month after Marie moved in, this home, too, was a mess. A hole had been kicked through one bedroom wall, and floors were strewn with boxes, clothes and litter.

Marie must pay for her electricity, water and phone. She complains that welfare does not pay her enough. "By the end of the month, my money is totally gone."

"I love all my kids," Marie says, but admits her turbulent life has "damaged" them. Her first husband took custody of her first four children. The oldest, now 29, "doesn't want anything to do with me." She has no idea where her second child is and has seen her third only once since he was two. That visit lasted less than 30 minutes.

Marie's fourth was placed in a foster home at ten months. "They have raised him and, thank God, he has done better than any of my children," she says. She has heard he is a high-school graduate and is in the Navy.

Her fifth child, Valerie, "caused problems because she's been jealous of one of the guys I've dated." (In 1988 Sam was jailed for sexually assaulting Valerie.) According to Marie, Valerie, now 19, has had one baby, who was surrendered for adoption. At last report, she lived in Wisconsin, was pregnant again and was still unmarried. Marie says the two have not spoken since Valerie struck her with a baseball bat.

Daughter Kelly has also struck her mother, with an iron candlestick. But Marie denies beating the children. "I hit them lightly on the mouth with the hand that doesn't have the ring on it, so I don't knock their teeth out," she says. At 16, Kelly has already borne two children out of wedlock. She is sure that her mother's example has influenced her. "A lot of what I've done is because of what I've seen," Kelly says.

When Marie moved to Germantown, she was eligible for $459 per month in food-stamp benefits and $521 in AFDC. But within days of that move, the four children living with her were taken away and placed in foster care because, Marie says, her 13-year-old son had sexually abused her six-year-old daughter. As a result, her AFDC was cut off and the food-stamp benefits were drastically reduced.

Marie vows to regain custody of the children. Meanwhile, might she get a job, as long as there are no children to look after and her AFDC payments have stopped? "Not really," she says, adding that her "health has deteriorated" and that she is beginning counseling. According to Marie, her Medicaid-supplied psychiatrist has told her she suffers from "stress." On a Friday afternoon, a departing visitor leaves her stretched out on the sofa amid the disarray of her home, watching cartoons.

Marie's youngest child, still in foster care, is only six. Will she continue in the footsteps of her grandmother, her mother and her older sisters? Welfare is all the child has ever known. "She talks about boyfriends now," Marie says. "She had her doll inside of her shirt playing like she was going to be a mommy."

Cindy K.

The one-bedroom apartment off a strip mall in Carmichael, Calif., has almost no furniture except for a bed, an old couch and a table. Just one picture—a movie poster—decorates the wall. But it is home to Cindy K., age 17, and her two sons. The boys have different fathers, and she has never married.

At 20 months, Alex sleeps through the night, but Cyrus, at four months, wakes up as many as five times. Two such young children would be a handful for even a mature woman, and Cindy is far from mature. Sometimes she finds herself yelling at them—"the littlest thing will snap me." Sometimes, "when both of them are crying at me," she shuts herself in the bathroom.

Cindy says she had the first baby on purpose, for "someone to love me." By the second baby, she knew better and talked, during her pregnancy, about putting the child up for adoption. The baby's father refused, however, even though at 27 he already had six other children by three other women.

Cindy and her children are living as they are because of welfare. Without it, she says, she would have surrendered not just the second child but both of her children for adoption. Because welfare was available, she enrolled and it falls to her to see that they "have a better life than I did."

Reprinted with permission: Tribune Media Services.

It is a daunting task for which she has been ill-prepared. Like her sons, Cindy was born out of wedlock and raised on welfare. Her father has never been part of her life. Her mother, Beverly, abused liquor and drugs. Says Beverly, "I was teaching Cindy to roll joints when she was six years old." With her mother often absent, Cindy was left to raise two younger siblings. Cindy says she was sexually molested between the ages of four and six by three different men. These experiences intensified the loneliness and anchorlessness of her life.

When Cindy was 14, her family moved into an apartment building inhabited by tough teen-age kids. As her mother's drug abuse intensified, Cindy dropped out of school and fell in with a bad crowd.

Soon she became distraught over a boyfriend who had been unfaithful. A 17-year-old, with beautiful green eyes that she noticed right away, spoke kindly to her and asked to be her new boyfriend. Cindy said yes.

When she learned that he was using drugs, she cried. "I didn't want him to be like my mom," she says, "but then I accepted it." For a while she used drugs too.

But Cindy preferred to drink. Her first sexual experience occurred in such a fog of alcohol that she scarcely remembers the occasion.

By the time Alex was born, two weeks before her 16th birthday, Cindy and her boyfriend had broken up. She and Alex lived with her mother and received their welfare payments through her grant. Cindy wanted to leave her mother's house, but didn't quite have the nerve. "I wanted to be an adult, and my mom was treating me like a kid," she explains. "She had rules on me, and I didn't want to follow them."

Even though she had her own baby, Cindy again felt terribly lonely. When Alex was five months old, she met a man who worked in construction, and she became pregnant again.

After Cyrus's birth, her fights with her mother worsened. Cindy found an apartment and arranged for welfare to pay the rent. Last August, she set up housekeeping on her own.

Cindy gets $607 per month in AFDC, out of which the welfare office pays her $380 rent directly and sends her the balance. She gets Medicaid and $216 worth of food stamps. It is hard to make ends meet.

Cyrus's father comes to see her and his son a few times a week. Alex's father takes him for an occasional weekend, but she cannot count on him. Cindy loves Cyrus's father and still has "feelings" for Alex's father. But lately she is a little angry at both of them. "I wasn't alone when these kids were made, but I'm here to do everything by myself," she says. "Sometimes I just get real mad. '

Alex, a strong, husky boy, is in constant motion. He fills the room with unceasing clamor, pawing his mother for the cookies and orange soda she is having for lunch. He and the baby both have runny noses, and often their faces go unwiped.

Cindy attends a high school for teen-age mothers. She hopes to graduate this year, then enter trade school to become a secretary. Her high school offers day care. Who will mind her children while she attends trade school and works? She hasn't "thought that far ahead yet."

At school, she keeps mostly to herself. After school she feeds the boys, bathes them, eats dinner and tries to do her homework.

A tall young woman with a pretty face, Cindy is thin and looks exhausted, speaking barely above a whisper when at all. She says she knows she can make it because "I'm doing it now."

But she claims she doesn't want to remain on welfare and wants to be married someday. She adds candidly, "I know it's not right what I'm doing. It makes me scared because I could go to hell."

Denise B.

Denise B., 29, is a strong-looking woman of medium height with a confident walk and, when necessary, a tough, wary manner. She lives in a "lock-down building" in Chicago's Harold Ickes Homes, a public-housing project run by the federally funded Chicago Housing Authority and monitored around the clock by armed guards.

Denise has five daughters, ages one to 13. All, after the first, were conceived on welfare—conceived perhaps deliberately. "I can't say in the back of my mind that I didn't want them," she says, chuckling. "I like big families, and you don't make five mistakes." How did she imagine she would care for her children when she had no job and repeatedly became pregnant? "That's where the public aid comes in," Denise replies.

Once Denise was a B student at Chicago's Holy Angels School, a well-regarded parochial school. She and her three younger siblings were raised by a mother and stepfather who both had good jobs, owned their own home and sacrificed to pay private-school tuition. Her parents would later separate, but Denise describes her childhood as "normal."

When she was 11, however, Denise met Joe, a schoolmate two years her senior. Joe lived in public housing with his grandmother, two siblings and, off and on, their unmarried mother, Roberta. Although Roberta says she worked steadily, Joe's grandmother helped support the children with AFDC checks.

Denise became pregnant in 1981, when she was 15. No one urged the teen-agers to marry, but Denise and Joe themselves had what she calls a "family-time talk" about making a commitment and raising their children together. What happened to those plans is something like what happened to her other plan, way back then, to continue her studies and become a lawyer. "It just slips away if you don't stay with it," she says. "It slips away."

Five months into the pregnancy, Denise signed up for welfare. Says Roberta matter-of-factly, "She was of an age to get her own money." Denise dropped out of school and never went back. Soon after her first daughter was born, Denise and the baby moved in with Joe and his grandmother.

Both Joe and Denise have been in jail. In the past 14 years, Joe has been charged with 50 crimes, including domestic battery, theft, and drug dealing, committed under his own name and eight aliases. He contracted lupus, an often debilitating disease, and began collecting Social Security, which now totals $443 a month.

Before she was 18, Denise worked sporadically in a series of fast-food jobs. But when her second child was born, in 1984, "working wasn't an issue anymore," she says.

Joe's grandmother died a year later, and Roberta became head of her household. In 1989, she won legal custody of Denise's and Joe's three children.

In 1991, Denise ended up in jail for shoplifting. She was also pregnant. When her jail term was over, she moved into a two-bedroom apartment in the Ickes project with the new baby. Her fifth child was born in 1993.

Last fall, authorities took away her two youngest children. They, too, are with Roberta and, like the other three, are supported by over $2000 per month in grants from the Illinois Department of Child and Family Services.

Today Denise says she is trying to get her children back. Before they were taken away, the government paid her $331 per month in AFDC, $212 in food stamps and gave her Medicaid. Her subsidized rent is $89 per month, and she pays no utilities. Without children she is ineligible for AFDC cash grants. In the interim she is looking into other assistance programs.

Denise says she would like to work. But she'd have to earn a lot, she says, for it to be a better deal than welfare. "You've got to look at the medical, the food and everything else," she says. Besides, to get a good job, she would first have to go to school, then earn her way up to a high salary. "That's going to take time," she says. "It's a lot of work, and I ain't guaranteed to get nothing." She'd have to struggle to do well on the job. Welfare, by contrast, *is* guaranteed—"until they cut it out, until they say no more." Denise knows politicians are talking about that now and says she does not believe they are wrong. "We don't want to set no trend in this family that we all go down this public-aid line," she says.

So far, though, that *is* the family trend. Denise's brother is employed, but her 23- and 24-year-old sisters have both been on welfare for years and are also unwed mothers. One sister has five children; the other has three.

Denise has not talked to her sisters about how they came to live as adults so differently from the way they lived as children. There is no reason to. "I know what happened to them, and they know what happened to me." Welfare, she offers, "is an enabler. It's not that you want to be in that situation. But it's there. We always know."

Who are the greatest victims of welfare? Certainly, both taxpayers and recipients suffer. But as these portraits show, no one suffers more than the children. As the national debate on reform turns to legislation, the faces of welfare's victims should not be forgotten.

"The statistics haven't changed much over the years: women still use welfare to support their families when their children are small."

Welfare Is a Necessity for Some Women

Rita Henley Jensen

Welfare advocates argue that the majority of recipients spend only a short time in the system and do not abuse the benefits. In the following viewpoint, Rita Henley Jensen describes her own experience as a welfare mother and the difficulties she encountered while raising two children on the limited aid she received. She maintains that the typical aid recipient is a white mother of two—such as herself—rather than the stereotypical "black welfare queen" portrayed by politicians and the media. Jensen is an investigative journalist in New York City.

As you read, consider the following questions:

1. According to Jensen, why did she enroll in a class on the economics of public policy?
2. In the author's opinion, what explains the current urgency for tax cuts and spending reductions?
3. What do reporters focus on when they write about welfare, according to the author?

Excerpted from Rita Henley Jensen, "Welfare: Exploding the Stereotypes," *Ms.*, July/August 1995. Reprinted by permission of *Ms.* magazine; ©1995.

I am a woman. A white woman, once poor but no longer. I am not lazy, never was. I am a middle-aged woman, with two grown daughters. I was a welfare mother, one of those women society considers less than nothing.

I should have applied for Aid to Families with Dependent Children (AFDC) when I was eighteen years old, pregnant with my first child, and living with a boyfriend who slapped me around. But I didn't.

I remember talking it over at the time with a friend. I lived in the neighborhood that surrounds the vast Columbus campus of Ohio State University. Students, faculty, hangers-on, hippies, runaways, and recent émigrés from Kentucky lived side by side in the area's relatively inexpensive housing. I was a runaway.

The Decision to Go On Welfare

On a particularly warm midsummer's day, I stood on High Street, directly across from the campus' main entrance, with an older, more sophisticated friend, wondering what to do with my life. With my swollen belly, all hope of my being able to cross the street and enroll in the university had evaporated. Now, I was seeking advice about how merely to survive, to escape the assaults and still be able to care for my child.

My friend knew of no place I could go, nowhere I could turn, no one else I could ask. I remember saying in a tone of resignation, "I can't apply for welfare." Instead of disagreeing with me, she nodded, acknowledging our mutual belief that taking beatings was better than taking handouts. Being "on the dole" meant you deserved only contempt.

In August 1965, I married my attacker.

Six years later, I left him and applied for assistance. My children were eighteen months and five and a half years old. I had waited much too long. Within a year, I crossed High Street to go to Ohio State. I graduated in four years and moved to New York City to attend Columbia University's Graduate School of Journalism. I have worked as a journalist for eighteen years now. My life on welfare was very hard—there were times when I didn't have enough food for the three of us. But I was able to get an education while on welfare. It is hardly likely that a woman on AFDC today would be allowed to do what I did, to go to school and develop the kinds of skills that enabled me to make a better life for myself and my children.

In the summer of 1994, I attended a conference in Chicago on feminist legal theory. During the presentation of a paper related to gender and property rights, the speaker mentioned as an aside that when one says "welfare mother" the listener hears "black welfare mother." A discussion ensued about the underlying racism until someone declared that the solution was easy:

all that had to be done was have the women in the room bring to the attention of the media the fact that white women make up the largest percentage of welfare recipients. At this point, I stood, took a deep breath, stepped out of my professional guise, and informed the crowd that I was a former welfare mother. Looking at my white hair, blue eyes, and freckled Irish skin, some laughed; others gasped—despite having just acknowledged that someone like me was, in fact, a "typical" welfare mother.

Speaking Up and Not Speaking Up

Occasionally I do this. Speak up. Identify myself as one of "them." I do so reluctantly because welfare mothers are a lightning rod for race hatred, class prejudice, and misogyny. Yet I am aware that as long as welfare is viewed as an *African American* woman's issue, instead of a *woman's* issue—whether that woman be white, African American, Asian, Latina, or Native American—those in power can continue to exploit our country's racism to weaken and even eliminate public support for the programs that help low-income mothers and their children.

I didn't have the guts to stand up during a 1974 reception for Ohio state legislators. The party's hostess was a leader of the Columbus chapter of the National Organization for Women and she had opened up her suburban home so that representatives of many of the state's progressive organizations could lobby in an informal setting for an increase in the state's welfare allotment for families. I was invited as a representative of the campus area's single mothers' support group. In the living room, I came across a state senator in a just-slightly-too-warm-and-friendly state induced by the potent combination of free booze and a crowd of women. He quickly decided I looked like a good person to amuse with one of his favorite jokes. "You want to know how a welfare mother can prevent getting pregnant?" he asked, giggling. "She can just take two aspirin—and put them between her knees," he roared, as he bent down to place his Scotch glass between his own, by way of demonstration. I drifted away.

I finally did gather up my courage to speak out. It was in a classroom during my junior year. I was enrolled in a course on the economics of public policy because I wanted to understand why the state of Ohio thought it desirable to provide me and my two kids with only $204 per month—59 percent of what even the state itself said a family of three needed to live.

For my required oral presentation, I chose "Aid to Families with Dependent Children." I cited the fact that approximately two-thirds of all the pool families in the country were white: I noted that most welfare families consisted of one parent and two children. As an audiovisual aid, I brought my own two kids along. My voice quavered a bit as I delivered my intro: I stood with my arms around my children and said, "We are a typical AFDC family."

My classmates had not one question when I finished. I don't believe anyone even bothered to ask the kids' names or ages.

Declining Levels of Support

If I were giving this talk today, I would hold up a picture of us back then and say we still represent typical welfare recipients. The statistics I would cite to back up that statement have been refined since the 1970s and now include "Hispanic" as a category. In 1992, 38.9 percent of all welfare mothers were white, 37.2 percent were black, 17.8 percent were "Hispanic," 2.8 percent were Asian, and 1.4 percent were Native American.

My report, however, would focus on the dramatic and unrelenting reduction in resources available to low-income mothers in the last two decades.

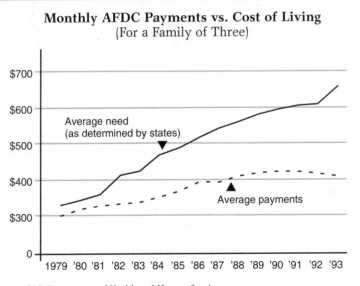

Monthly AFDC Payments vs. Cost of Living
(For a Family of Three)

Source: U.S. Department of Health and Human Services.

Fact: In 1970, the average monthly benefit for a family of three was $178. Not much, but consider that as a result of inflation, that $178 would be approximately $680 today. And then consider that the average monthly payment today is only about $414. That's the way it's been for more than two decades: the cost of living goes up (by the states' own accounting, the cost of rent, food, and utilities for a family of three has doubled), but the real value of welfare payments keeps going down.

Fact: The 1968 Work Incentive Program (the government called it WIN; we called it WIP) required that all unemployed adult recipients sign up for job training or employment once their children turned six. The age has now been lowered to three, and states may go as low as age one. What that means is you won't be able to attend and finish college while on welfare. (In most states a college education isn't considered job training, even though experts claim most of us will need college degrees to compete in the workplace of the twenty-first century.)

Fact: Forty-two percent of welfare recipients will be on welfare less than two years during their entire lifetime, and an additional 33 percent will spend between two and eight years on welfare. The statistics haven't changed much over the years: women still use welfare to support their families when their children are small.

In 1974, I ended my talk with this joke: A welfare mother went into the drugstore and bought a can of deodorant. I explained that it was funny because everyone knew that welfare mothers could not afford "extras" like personal hygiene products. My joke today would be: A welfare mother believed that if elected public officials understood these facts, they would not campaign to cut her family's benefits.

The idea that government representatives care about welfare mothers is as ridiculous to me now as the idea back then that I would waste my limited funds on deodorant. It is much clearer to me today what the basic functions of welfare public policy are at this moment in U.S. history.

Politicians' War on Welfare Recipients

By making war on welfare recipients, political leaders can turn the public's attention away from the government's redistribution of wealth to the wealthy. Recent studies show that the United States has become the most economically stratified of industrial nations. In fact, Federal Reserve figures reveal that the richest 1 percent of American households—each with a minimum net worth of $2.3 million—controls nearly 40 percent of the wealth, while in Britain, the richest 1 percent of the population controls about 18 percent of the wealth. In the mid-1970s, both countries were on a par: the richest 1 percent controlled 20 percent of the wealth. President Reagan was the master of this verbal shell game. He told stories of welfare queens and then presided over the looting of the nation's savings and loans by wealthy white men.

Without a doubt, the current urgency for tax cuts and spending reductions can be explained by the fact that President Clinton tried to shift the balance slightly in 1992 and the wealthy ended up paying 16 percent more in taxes the following year, by one estimate.

The purpose of this antiwelfare oratory and the campaigns against sex education, abortion rights, and aid to teenage mothers is to ensure a constant supply of young women as desperate and ashamed as I was. Young women willing to take a job at any wage rate, willing to tolerate the most abusive relationships with men, and unable to enter the gates leading to higher education.

To accomplish their goals, political leaders continually call for reforms that include demands that welfare recipients work, that teenagers don't have sex, and that welfare mothers stop giving birth (but don't have abortions). Each "reform" addresses the nation's racial and sexual stereotypes: taking care of one's own children is not work; welfare mothers are unemployed, promiscuous, and poorly motivated; and unless the government holds their feet to the fire, these women will live on welfare for years as will their children and their children's children.

This type of demagoguery has been common throughout our history. What sets the present era apart is the nearly across-the-board cooperation of the media. The national news magazines, the most prestigious daily newspapers, the highly regarded broadcast news outlets, as well as the supermarket tabloids and talk-radio hosts, have generally abandoned the notion that one of their missions is to sometimes comfort the afflicted and afflict the comfortable. Instead, they too often reprint politicians' statements unchallenged, provide charts comparing one party's recommendations to another's without really questioning those recommendations, and illustrate story after story, newscast after newscast, with a visual of an African American woman (because we all know they're the only ones on welfare) living in an urban housing project (because that's where all welfare recipients live) who has been on welfare for years.

The Media's Image of Welfare Women

When *U.S. News & World Report* did a major story on welfare reform in January 1995, it featured large photographs of eight welfare recipients, seven of whom were women of color: six African Americans and one Latina or Native American (the text does not state her ethnicity). Describing the inability of welfare mothers to hold jobs (they are "hobbled not only by their lack of experience but also by their casual attitudes toward punctuality, dress, and coworkers"), the article offers the "excuse" given by one mother for not taking a 3 P.M. to 11 P.M. shift: "I wouldn't get to see my kids," she told the reporter. You can't win for losing—should she take that 3-to-11 job and her unsupervised kids get in trouble, you can be sure some conservative would happily leap on her as an example of one of those poor women who are bad mothers and whose kids should be in orphanages.

Why don't the media ever find a white woman from Ohio or Iowa or Wisconsin, a victim of domestic violence, leaving the father of her two children to make a new start? Or a Latina mother like the one living in my current neighborhood, who has one child and does not make enough as a home health care attendant to pay for her family's health insurance? Or a Native American woman living on a reservation, creating crafts for pennies that will be sold by others for dollars?

Besides reinforcing stereotypes about the personal failings of welfare recipients, when my colleagues write in-depth pieces about life on welfare they invariably concentrate on describing welfare mothers' difficulties with the world at large: addictions, lack of transportation, dangerous neighbors, and, most recently, shiftless boyfriends who begin beating them when they do get jobs—as if this phenomenon were limited to relationships between couples with low incomes.

I wonder why no journalist I have stumbled across, no matter how well meaning, has communicated what I believe is the central reality of most women's lives on welfare: they believe all the stereotypes too and they are ashamed of being on welfare. They eat, breathe, sleep, and clothe themselves with shame. . . .

Welfare "Fraud"

On welfare, I had to prove every statement was not a lie. Everything had to be documented: how many children I had, how much I paid for rent, fuel, transportation, electricity, child care, and so forth. It went so far as to require that at every "redetermination of need" interview (every six months), I had to produce the originals of my children's birth certificates, which were duly photocopied over and over again. Since birth certificates do not change, the procedure was a subtle and constant reminder that nothing I said was accepted as truth. Ever.

But this is a petty example. The more significant one was the suspicion that my attendance at Ohio State University was probably a crime. Throughout my college years, I regularly reported that I was attending OSU. Since the WIN limit at that time was age six and my youngest daughter was two when I started, I was allowed to finish my undergraduate years without having to report to some job-training program that would have prepared me for a minimum-wage job. However, my caseworker and I shared an intuitive belief that something just had to be wrong about this. How could I be living on welfare and going to college? Outrageous! Each day I awoke feeling as if I were in a race, that I had to complete my degree before I was charged with a felony.

As a matter of fact, I remember hearing, a short time after I graduated, that a group of welfare mothers attending college in Ohio were charged with food stamp fraud, apparently for not reporting their scholarships as additional income. . . .

Welfare Reform

None of this is ever discussed in the context of welfare reform. The idiot state legislator, the prosecutor in Ohio who brought the charges against welfare mothers years ago, Bill Clinton, and Newt Gingrich all continue to play the race and sex card by hollering for welfare reform. They continue to exploit and feed the public's ignorance about and antipathy toward welfare mothers to propel their own careers. Sadly, journalists permit them to do so, perhaps for the same reason.

Lost in all this are the lives of thousands of women impoverished by virtue of their willingness to assume the responsibility of raising their children. An ex-boyfriend used to say that observing my struggle was a little like watching someone standing in a room, with arms upraised to prevent the ceiling from pressing in on her. He wondered just how long I could prevent the collapse.

Today, welfare mothers have even less opportunity than I did. Their talent, brains, luck, and resourcefulness are ignored. Each new rule, regulation, and reform makes it even more unlikely that they can use the time they are on welfare to do as I did: cross the High Streets in their cities and towns, and realize their ambitions. Each new rule makes it more likely that they will only be able to train for a minimum-wage job that will never allow them to support their families.

So no, I don't think all we have to do is get the facts to the media. I think we have to raise hell any way we can.

Our goal is simple: never again should there be a young woman, standing in front of the gates that lead to a better future, afraid to enter because she believes she must instead choose poverty and battery.

"Welfare caseloads grew by 30 percent between 1991 and 1994 in part because many dads were not supporting their children."

Noncustodial Fathers Should Be Required to Support Their Children

Paul Offner

Many welfare reformers maintain that since abandonment of families by fathers is the main reason for the high number of welfare cases, the costs of the programs would be reduced if "deadbeat dads" were forced to support their children. In the following viewpoint, Paul Offner argues that states already have a financial incentive to pursue fathers who fail to pay child support, but they do not have the technical means to do so. To help the states, he proposes, the Internal Revenue Service could collect support from fathers who abandon their children. Offner is a legislative aide to New York senator Daniel Patrick Moynihan.

As you read, consider the following questions:

1. According to Offner, what amount should have been collected in 1994 for child support?
2. By what percentage did collection of child support increase between 1983 and 1992, according to the author?
3. What is the national objective of the Aid to Families with Dependent Children program, in the author's view?

Paul Offner, "Kid Stuff," *New Republic*, August 1, 1994. Reprinted by permission of the *New Republic*, ©1994, The New Republic, Inc.

During the 1992 campaign Bill Clinton railed at deadbeat dads who don't pay child support. "We'll garnish your wages, we'll suspend your license, we'll track you across state lines and, if necessary, we'll make some of you work off what you owe," he warned. So far, however, the president's threats have yielded few results. The Department of Health and Human Services (HHS) reports that of the $47 billion in child support that should be collected in 1994, only $13 billion actually will be paid. If history is any guide, many of the people who get stiffed will end up on welfare, which is why the Clinton welfare reform proposal, like others before it, includes tougher child support enforcement. The trouble is, it may not be tough enough.

There are many reasons why the current system isn't working: the failure to fully automate child support records; turf fights between state, county and local court officials. But the main reason is that the states haven't devoted the necessary resources to enforcement. "There is simply not enough staff working in the program," says a report by the Commission on Interstate Child Support. Ideally, a child support caseworker would have 300 cases; instead, the average caseworker today has at least 1,000 cases, according to the General Accounting Office. This understaffing occurs even though the federal government funds more than 80 percent of the program—and even though the states have an incentive to do better. When child support owed to welfare recipients is collected, welfare payments are reduced. Most large, northern states get to keep half of the resulting savings, so for every dollar they invest in child support enforcement, they save at least that much in welfare costs. Last year alone, thanks to this arrangement, the states pocketed $475 million.

Why States Don't Pursue Deadbeats

Why don't states invest more? One problem is that child support programs are often buried in state welfare departments, so many governors and legislators don't see their money-making potential. In addition, the rules handed down by federal child support bureaucrats are so detailed and inflexible that they impede state collection efforts. They dictate how fast money coming in to a child support office must go out, how fast information collected by the staff must be passed on to caseworkers and what forms must be filled out. They mandate that 75 percent of all cases must be "worked" in an audit period, whether that accomplishes anything or not. The emphasis is on process rather than product—and it shows. Between 1983 and 1992 the percentage of cases in which state agencies collected child support increased only slightly, from 14.7 to 18.7. At that rate, it will be the year 2062 before we make collections in *half* the cases.

To repair the system—to hold states accountable for lax

enforcement—that emphasis should be reversed. "Audits should focus more on program effectiveness than on simple compliance with processes," Reagan HHS Secretary Margaret Heckler argued in 1983. The current secretary, Donna Shalala, agrees. The states say they agree, too, but it's hard to tell if they mean it. When former Representative Tom Downey of New York chaired the Welfare Subcommittee of the House Ways and Means Committee, he issued a report comparing states' success at collecting child support. The states howled. State child support directors claimed that you can't make such comparisons because states differ in areas such as income and population. Asked to grade the federal government's performance on Downey's 1991 report card, the states gave child support bureaucrats a C. Downey, in turn, gave the states a D.

Identifying Fathers in the Welfare Debate

A great deal of attention is paid to welfare moms; they are the subject of endless scrutiny and demagoguery and sermonizing. They are asked to be both mother and father, to raise children responsibly in often dangerous neighborhoods while finding some way to become self-sufficient.

But what about the dads? It's almost as if all these unfortunate conceptions were immaculate. The fathers, in most (66 percent of all out-of-wedlock) cases, are never identified. And, if identified, they are almost never forced to be responsible for their acts. Only 18 percent pay child support. This is a remarkable scandal.

Joe Klein, *Newsweek*, June 21, 1993.

This finger-pointing suggests that the biggest problem is not just with child support, but with all social welfare programs run jointly by the federal government and the states, including Aid to Families with Dependent Children (AFDC) and Medicaid. The two sides are constantly at each other's throats, and millions of dollars are wasted on unnecessary audits and lawsuits. Medicare, by contrast, is administered entirely by the federal government and operates smoothly, with little controversy (apart from complaints by doctors and hospitals that they are not paid enough). In AFDC's case, joint administration may be unavoidable, since national objectives (providing a safety net) must be balanced against local ones (encouraging work, holding down local costs). But that is not the case with child support enforcement, where the objectives are broadly shared.

The president hopes to remedy all this in his welfare bill. He proposes comprehensive reforms—"the toughest child support enforcement measures in the history of this country," he says. Fathers who don't pay child support would lose any professional or occupational licenses they hold, as well as their driver's licenses. Mothers who don't cooperate in tracking down the father of their children would be denied benefits. Every state would have to create a central registry of child support orders to help find delinquent, deserting dads. And the new system would be based on performance rather than process.

The administration believes that these and other changes can turn the system around. Maybe so. But if the results haven't improved dramatically within, say, five years, we should federalize child support and run it as an adjunct to the tax system. No longer would delinquent fathers be able to avoid their obligations by moving to another state. Child support would become a federal obligation on a par with income taxes; the Internal Revenue Service (IRS) could go after deadbeats. Moreover, it would be up to Congress, not the states, to make sure that the program was adequately staffed.

Critics of federalizing the program say it runs counter to the current enthusiasm for decentralization, and that it won't fix all the problems of the local court systems. That's true; many local courts have huge backlogs and delays. Yet federalization will streamline the rest of the system. The IRS is also unenthusiastic about the idea, believing that it would inherit a whole new set of administrative headaches. That's also true—but the IRS is more competent to deal with these problems than fifty competing, poorly staffed state governments.

The fact is, we can't continue along our present path. Welfare caseloads grew by 30 percent between 1991 and 1994 in part because many dads were not supporting their children. With the exception of a few states (Delaware, Michigan, Washington), the child support system isn't working. If we truly mean to reform welfare, we'll have to fix it.

"Eventually, society may learn to distinguish between responsible fathers and 'deadbeat dads.'"

Most Noncustodial Fathers Support Their Children

Jenifer Rachel

Some reformers contend that the number of welfare recipients has increased because "deadbeat dads" are not supporting their children. In the following viewpoint, Jenifer Rachel maintains that the majority of fathers do support their children. State and federal efforts to collect child support do not increase benefits for children, she argues, since most of the money is kept by the state or is used by the custodial mother for other purposes. Furthermore, she says, the system indiscriminately infringes upon the rights of fathers and harms the relationship between fathers and children. Rachel is a freelance writer in Helendale, California.

As you read, consider the following questions:

1. How much money does a child receive when the state collects $600 in child support from his or her father, according to Rachel?
2. According to Census Bureau figures cited by the author, in what percentage of cases is child support paid in full?
3. What percentage of fathers with joint custody of their children pay child support, as reported by the Census Bureau and cited by the author?

Jenifer Rachel, "They're Not All 'Deadbeat Dads.'" This article appeared in the April 1994 issue and is reprinted with permission from the *World & I*, a publication of The Washington Times Corporation; copyright ©1994.

Media hype continues to unduly propagate images of stereotypical "deadbeat dads": wealthy men who leave poverty-stricken children with no means of support. Policymakers and special-interest groups perpetuate their causes by providing the media with inaccurate data. Child support is no longer strictly for children; states are profiting from child-support collections while children remain in poverty. Support awards are skyrocketing; visitation rights are not enforced; and male custody is virtually unattainable, leaving man's primary role as a cash donor. The Clinton administration has turned a deaf ear to over sixteen million fathers who live in households without their children while responding to pressure from lobbyists on the other side of the fence.

In 1988 the federal Office of Child Support Enforcement (OCSE) passed the Family Support Act (FSA) requiring states to comply with federal child-support guidelines. As a result, stringent enforcement techniques allow government to intrude on the lives of male citizens with the implementation of wage assignments, tax-refund intercepts, liens, and interest penalties on arrearages.

Current policy is designed to allow children to remain at the same economic levels they enjoyed before their parents were divorced, placing unrealistic demands on noncustodial parents. In today's society, men bear the brunt of responsibility for maintaining children's economic lifestyles, and additional pressure arises when the custodial mother is a "deadbeat." When a mother cannot work, or chooses not to, the father and taxpayers are required to pay the entire bill.

How Much Is Enough?

"Collecting child support is the cornerstone of both federal and state deliberations on welfare reform," according to the National Conference of State Legislatures (NCSL). It admits, however, that "although the child-support program is generally attached to a social welfare agency, legislators increasingly treat child support in the same fashion as other state revenue-collection agencies." San Bernardino District Attorney Dennis Kottmeier states, "The significance of child support is that it's a money-maker."

States gain because the federal government pays 66 percent of state and local administrative costs for services to those on Aid to Families with Dependent Children (AFDC). In addition to federal reimbursement for administrative costs, states also receive federal incentive payments. Simply put, the more child support a state collects, the greater its federal return.

Unfortunately, it is not the children who benefit from the states' collections when the mother is on AFDC. The children receive a flat $50 of the money sent by their parent; the remainder is considered "welfare reimbursement" and is split between the state and federal governments. Therefore, a child whose father is paying $600 a month receives the same $50 as the child whose father is paying $150. The government intercepts the remaining $550 and $100, respectively. Therefore, incentive is high for states to get their hands in the pockets of those earning high wages; because success is measured in dollars collected, it is most rewarding for caseworkers to pursue responsible working men whose paychecks are easily attainable. True deadbeats are not considered "cost effective" and often escape.

Child Support Money Spent by the State

In 1987, the fifty states gained revenues of $663 million directly from fathers with children on AFDC and from federal incentive payments, which they were free to spend at their discretion. In Florida, a special trust fund for children's services was established in 1987 using revenues generated from the child-support program. Other revenues have been linked to programs to fight child abuse and neglect and to early childhood education programs. Although the worthiness of these programs goes uncontested, should child-support monies be spent on anything other than the specific children for whom they were meant?

The Crusade Against "Deadbeat Dads"

One type of at-risk child is becoming more and more common in America: the child living with only one parent. . . .

Fortunately for those leading a dramatic crusade against this growing trend, there's a villain to blame: the deadbeat dad. Fathers across the United States are abandoning their families and their financial responsibilities in ever-growing numbers, the story goes, and only the government—more and more only the *federal* government—has the power to stop them.

The government has been trying. But it just might be hitting a dead end. Its attempts to do better seem more and more a quick skid down a faster road to serfdom than even [the economist] F.A. Hayek envisioned—and some of its efforts seem more inclined toward helping itself than helping children.

Brian Doherty, *Reason*, June 1996.

California has been the highest ranked state in mandated money transfers between parents since its Civil Code 4721 went into effect July 1, 1992. The average amount of support for two children in California is now $1,154 per month. Dave Whitman, corporate president and founder of the Coalition of Parent Support, a California-based political action group, says, "The significance is that California has often been in the forefront of family law and may set precedents for other states to follow." The coalition's primary interest is the repeal of Civil Code 4721. Its goal is not to avoid child support but to gain support orders that are fair to all parties involved.

Research in 1992 from the U.S. Department of Agriculture's Family Economics Research Group repudiates the view that such large support amounts are necessary. The research shows that two-parent families making $32,100 or less spend $331 a month on one child and $529 on two, exclusive of medical and child care; but current support orders in most states exceed this amount. No government regulations exist regarding the proper disbursement of child-support funds by custodial mothers, and, often, fathers feel that the mothers are benefiting personally from the payments. Robert, twenty-seven, an Ohio fireman, says, "I have no control over how my ex-wife spends the money I send. After having my payments increased by $300 per month, my ex-wife bought herself a brand-new car."

Accurate Statistics Needed

Mark Twain once said, "There are lies, damn lies, and then there are statistics," which accurately describes the child-support situation. The most widely cited statistics are those compiled by the Census Bureau, which report that child support is paid in full 50 percent of the time, in part 25 percent, and never 25 percent. But the figures reported by the Census Bureau do not reflect the reality of child-support compliance: The bureau asked only the custodial mothers whether payment had been received. It did not compare those responses with noncustodial fathers' reports of how much was paid or court records of how much was owed.

At one point, the federal government conducted a Survey of Absent Parents (SOAP) through the Health and Human Services Department (HHS) to learn more about obligated fathers. The results from that pilot survey undercut the stereotypes and the institutional desires of the OCSE. Wayne Stanton, then the administrator of the Family Support Administration and head of the child-support enforcement effort, killed the study and refused to publish the results. SOAP revealed that noncustodial fathers reported paying 10 to 40 percent more child support than the mothers said they paid. According to SOAP, compliance was clearly affected by the fact that as much as one-half of the absent parents were poor. In conclusion, SOAP asserted that child-support payments have quite possibly been systematically underestimated in the major data bases.

Clearly, delinquencies do exist, but the reasons do not parallel those reported by the media and special-interest groups. Sanford Braver, professor of psychology at Arizona State University, reported that unemployment is the strongest predictor of payment as yet identified. Further evidence appeared during a study performed by the Institute for Research on Poverty at the University of Wisconsin-Madison, which found that 80 percent of the Wisconsin paternity cases delinquent in child-support payments made less than $6,155 per year (below the single-person poverty line). Such findings are not conducive to the stereotype of the man in the Mercedes who refuses to support his children.

The Father-Child Relationship

Although the OCSE touts its enforcement successes under the guise of caring for children, many youths are being denied access to their fathers; the same legislatures that so heartily back child-support enforcement are refusing to act on behalf of the father-child relationship. The Children's Rights Council (CRC), a national child-advocacy organization, estimates that over six million children are having their visitation denied or interfered with by the custodial parent. During a recent interview, Eric Anderson, national coordinator for the CRC and member of the Texas Supreme Court Commission on Child Support and Access, said, "States have a very strong financial incentive to secure child support, but because there is no financial incentive to assure emotional support [visitation], this issue has been disregarded. It gets even tougher when the kids live in another state."

Previous policy required a custodial mother to petition the court before being permitted to relocate to another state and remove a child from the father. New laws do not mandate mothers to show just cause for moving, and, in many states, fathers have no legal right to stop them. Experts agree that children who grow up without a father show higher rates of delinquency, drug and alcohol abuse, teen pregnancy, and running away than do children of intact families, but Congress continues to pass legislation that belittles the importance of paternal involvement.

Although a positive correlation between visitation rights and child-support payments exists, the administration has proposed no action. The Census Bureau reported in 1989 that 90.2 percent of fathers with joint custody pay, as do 79.1 percent of fathers whose access is protected by a visitation order.

Steps to Reform

If true equity is to be gained between mothers, fathers, and children, the Clinton administration and Congress need to appoint commissions that are nonpartisan and not inclined to advocate on behalf of custodial parents alone; fathers must be represented in the policy process as well. The federal government should mandate accountability for the expenditure of the child-support check (as is currently done for Social Security benefits received on behalf of a child), thereby protecting children from those irresponsible mothers who spend child-support monies for personal gain.

True welfare reform would require mothers who are receiving aid to work if they are physically able to do so, relieving the father and taxpayer from sole support of the children. Also, legislation should be passed assuring children the right to both parents; joint custody and shared parenting provide emotional security for kids and have proved successful in child-support compliance. Finally, Congress should not pass more enforcement initiatives until the false stereotypes and misguided data have been corrected; then, its actions can be based on truth.

State agencies should provide legal aid for custodial and noncustodial parents alike. Fathers should not be required to hire expensive attorneys while mothers receive free legal representation. States also have an obligation to both parents to provide equal funding and staff when addressing issues important to family law. Caseworkers, motivated strictly by incentive payments from the federal government, should be granted bonuses only for securing child support from a nonpayer, not for increasing collections from men with excellent payment records.

At present, custodial mothers are able to use this system for their own financial gain, and it is integrity only, not the law, that prevents them from taking their exes to the cleaners. Mothers also must realize that they are instrumental in encouraging the father-child relationship.

Noncustodial fathers today are faced with a hostile political and social environment. They must learn to cope with an unfair system while working together to create positive changes in family law. Letter-writing campaigns, meetings with legislators, and involvement in father's rights organizations are effective tools for dads who want to make a difference. Eventually, society may learn to distinguish between responsible fathers and "deadbeat dads."

> "Non-citizens today are among the fastest
> growing groups of welfare dependents."

Immigrants Should
Be Denied Welfare

Robert Rector and William F. Lauber

Social spending on immigrants is an unfair burden on U.S. taxpayers, Robert Rector and William F. Lauber argue in the following viewpoint. They contend that the generous benefits provided
by the U.S. welfare system attract the elderly of other countries,
encouraging them to immigrate. The economic well-being of elderly immigrants should be the responsibility of their families
and sponsors, Rector and Lauber assert. Rector is a senior policy
analyst and Lauber is a research associate at the Heritage Foundation, a conservative think tank in Washington, D.C.

As you read, consider the following questions:

1. According to Rector and Lauber, how many noncitizens
   received aid from the Supplemental Security Insurance (SSI)
   program in 1994?
2. In Norman Matloff's estimate, cited by the authors, what
   percentage of elderly immigrants in California received
   welfare in 1990?
3. From what country do the greatest number of aliens
   receiving SSI come, according to the authors?

Robert Rector and William F. Lauber, "Elderly Non-citizens on Welfare Will Cost the
American Taxpayer $328 Billion over the Next Decade," F.Y.I., no. 54/95, March 23, 1995.
Reprinted by permission of the Heritage Foundation.

The United States welfare system is rapidly becoming a deluxe retirement home for the elderly of other countries. This is because many individuals are now immigrating to the United States in order to obtain generous welfare that far exceeds programs available in their country of origin. Non-citizens today are among the fastest growing groups of welfare dependents.

In 1994, there were nearly 738,000 lawful non-citizen residents receiving aid from the Supplemental Security Insurance (SSI) program. This was up from 127,900 in 1982—a 580 percent increase in just twelve years. The overwhelming majority of non-citizen SSI recipients are elderly. Most apply for welfare within five years of arriving in the United States.

The data show that welfare is becoming a way of life for elderly immigrants. An analysis of elderly immigrants in California by Professor Norman Matloff of the University of California at Davis shows that 45 percent received cash welfare in 1990. Among Russian immigrants, the figure is 66 percent; among Chinese, 55 percent. Worse, the trend is accelerating. Recent immigrants are far more likely to become welfare dependents than those who arrived in the United States in earlier decades.

A Future Catastrophe

If current trends continue, the U.S. will have more than three million non-citizens on SSI [by 2005]. Without reform, the total cost of SSI and Medicaid benefits for elderly non-citizen immigrants will amount to over $328 billion over the next ten years. Annual SSI and Medicaid benefits for these individuals will reach over $67 billion in 2004.

Even with the implausible assumption that the current rapid increase of non-citizen recipients will halt and the number of elderly immigrants receiving benefits will remain at current levels, U.S. taxpayers would still pay over $127 billion over the next ten years for SSI and Medicaid benefits for resident aliens.

Immigration should be open to individuals who wish to come to the United States to work and be self-sufficient. America has opened its doors to those who seek opportunity. But immigration should not become an avenue to welfare dependence.

Congressional testimony by Dr. Matloff demonstrates that immigrants have a high degree of awareness of welfare policies and procedures. Besides word of mouth among immigrants, sources in foreign countries as well as the United States give advice on how to obtain welfare benefits. For example, *Zai Meiguo Sheng Huo Xu Zhi (What You Need to Know About Life in America)*, a publication sold in Taiwan and Hong Kong, and in Chinese bookstores in the U.S., includes a thirty-six-page guide to SSI and other welfare benefits. The largest-circulation Chinese-language newspaper in the U.S., *Shijie Ribao (World Journal)*, runs a regular "Dear Abby"-style advice column on SSI and other immigration-related matters.

Prudent restrictions on providing welfare to recent immigrants long has been part of the American tradition. Becoming a charge was grounds for deportation in the Massachusetts Bay colony even before the American Revolution. America's first immigration law, passed by Congress in 1882, instructed immigration officials to deport any person who, in their opinion, might become a public charge. Today, the Immigration and Nationality Act declares unequivocally: "any alien who, within five years after the date of entry, has become a public charge from causes not affirmatively shown to have arisen since entry is deportable." The problem is that this provision of the law is ignored.

Projected Costs for Resident Aliens (with Current Growth in Caseload)

	Number of Resident Aliens on SSI	SSI Recipient Cost Per Year	Total SSI Cost
1995	854,323	$5035	$ 4,301,517,493
1996	988,794	5186	5,127,933,637
1997	1,144,430	5342	6,113,122,503
1998	1,324,563	5502	7,287,587,825
1999	1,533,049	5667	8,687,693,773
2000	1,774,351	5837	10,356,790,876
2001	2,053,634	6012	12,346,558,253
2002	2,376,876	6192	14,718,603,717
2003	2,750,997	6378	17,546,371,301
2004	3,184,003	6570	20,917,415,248
Total			$107,403,594,626

Note: Average growth rate in caseload from 1982–1994 was 15.74% per year. Outyear projections are based on this figure. SSI costs per recipient were allowed to grow at the rate of inflation (3.0%).

Source: SSI costs from Committee on Ways and Means, U.S. House of Representatives, *Overview of Entitlement Programs: 1994 Green Book*, 1994.

The presence of large numbers of elderly immigrants on welfare is a violation of the spirit, and arguably the letter, of U.S. immigration law. The relatives who sponsored the entry of these individuals into the U.S. implicitly promised that the new immigrants would not become a burden to the U.S. taxpayer.

But many, if not most, sponsors are enrolling their elderly immigrant relatives on welfare soon after the end of the three-year waiting period. Once on SSI, there is every indication that these immigrants will remain on welfare indefinitely.

Sympathy for Refugees Should Not Include Welfare

Although many of the elderly non-citizens on SSI come from politically oppressive nations such as Cuba or the former Soviet Union, the majority do not. The single greatest number of aliens on SSI come from Mexico. Other nations, such as the Dominican Republic, India, South Korea, and the Philippines, also contribute large numbers of recipients.

Moreover, while Americans greatly sympathize with those individuals who have suffered from political oppression and economic failure inherent to communist regimes, U.S. welfare programs are not appropriate vehicles to redress that suffering, nor should they serve as a retirement program for these individuals. Just as the United States military cannot serve as a global policeman, U.S. welfare programs cannot serve as a global retirement system.

Most non-citizens on SSI lawfully admitted to the U.S. have relatives capable of supporting them. To have brought a relative to the U.S. in the first place, the sponsor must have demonstrated a capacity to support that relative. And most sponsors do, in fact, support their immigrant relatives for at least three years after their arrival. If SSI benefits for non-citizens were terminated, in most cases the family support which sustained the immigrant immediately after arrival in the U.S. simply would be resumed.

Just as Americans expect an absent parent to pay child support for his children, so they also must expect individuals who voluntarily bring elderly and near-elderly relatives to the U.S. to support those relatives fully. This obligation to support should be permanent and should not be limited to three or five years as under the current law. Under no circumstances should the cost of supporting elderly and near-elderly immigrants to the United States be passed to the general taxpayer.

*"The assertion that immigrants use more federal
social services than natives is completely false."*

Immigrants Are Not a Heavy Burden on the Welfare System

Julian L. Simon

In the following viewpoint, Julian L. Simon contends that spending on immigrants in programs for the poor, such as Medicaid and welfare, only slightly exceeds that for native-born citizens. However, he argues, in entitlement programs such as Social Security and Medicare, which benefit all citizens regardless of income, spending on native-born citizens far exceeds expenditures on immigrants. Welfare spending for immigrants presents a negligible cost to taxpayers, he concludes. Simon is a professor of business and management at the University of Maryland and a senior fellow at the Cato Institute, a conservative libertarian think tank in Washington, D.C.

As you read, consider the following questions:

1. In Simon's estimate, how much does the government spend on each native-born citizen per year?
2. What programs does the author say are by far the most expensive?
3. What is the main reason for the gap between the costs of social spending for immigrants and natives, in the author's opinion?

Julian L. Simon, "What Immigrants Really Cost," *San Diego Union-Tribune*, April 19, 1996, p. B-9. Reprinted by permission.

Critics of immigration are arguing that legal immigrants "live at taxpayers' expense" on welfare programs. Even the pro-immigration camp has now come to believe that government expenditures on recent immigrants are greater than expenditures on natives. But even under current law, the assertion that immigrants use more federal social services than natives is completely false.

It is true that expenditures commonly called "welfare" are about $150 per year greater per immigrant than per native, and they have always been higher. But the welfare expenditures are only a drop in the bucket of total government social outlays on both groups.

The relevant totals are roughly $3,800 for natives and $2,200 for immigrants—or $1,600 less per immigrant per year. The piddling welfare expenditures on immigrants are a very red herring in policy debate. Let's consider the elements in the graph that tell the story.

Narrow Welfare Expenditures

From census and other federal data, Rebecca Clark of the Urban Institute calculated expenditures for immigrants and natives on Aid to Families with Dependent Children (AFDC), food stamps, Supplemental Security Income (SSI) and general assistance.

Foreign-born persons have perhaps a 15 percent higher probability of obtaining those goods and services than do natives. From her data, I estimate that federal expenditures average $404 per year per immigrant, while the average native receives $260.

Those data for the early 1990s are shown at the base of the immigrant and native columns in the graph. The data on those four federal welfare programs do not, however, include most government payments to the elderly or expenditures for local public schooling.

Now let's go to the top of graph. Payments to the elderly. Social Security and Medicare, by far the most expensive government transfer programs, are paid mainly to natives. That is because immigrants typically arrive when they are young and healthy and also because older recent immigrants do not qualify for Social Security.

Those expenditures are difficult to estimate for immigrants because the payments differ greatly among age groups. Total federal expenditures of $305 billion in 1992 for Social Security and $133 billion for Medicare indicate expenditures per native and immigrant of $1,305 and $566, respectively.

The authoritative 1975 data suggest that the average expenditure per immigrant who arrived within the past twenty-five years

137

[since 1970] is less than a fifth of the average expenditure per native—say $261 and $113, respectively, for argument. (Some allowance for the public support of the immigrant aged is reflected in the relatively heavy SSI payments that substitute for Social Security.) In the graph, those programs dwarf welfare programs.

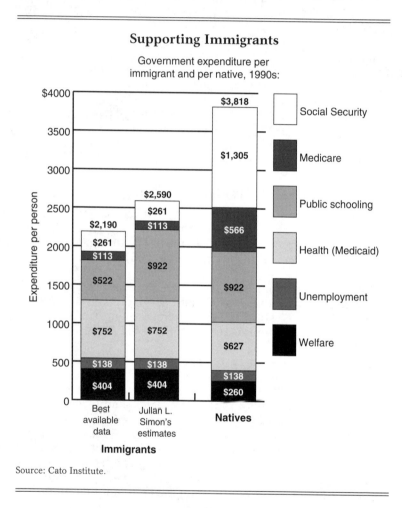

Supporting Immigrants

Government expenditure per
immigrant and per native, 1990s:

Source: Cato Institute.

Schooling costs. Clark's estimates imply $522 per capita for immigrants and $922 per capita for natives. The expenditures are lower for the immigrant population because the proportion of children is a smaller proportion of the total immigrant population than of the total native population. I consider it prudent, however, to assume schooling costs for immigrants equal to those of natives; both estimates are shown in the graph.

138

Unemployment compensation. We can safely assume similar expenditures of $138 per capita for immigrants and natives, based on earlier solid data.

Medicaid. It is reasonable to assume higher expenditures for immigrants than for natives, because immigrants are somewhat poorer on average than natives. Federal and state Medicaid expenditures are about $90 billion and $70 billion, respectively, so expenditures per person are about $627 for natives and perhaps $752 for immigrants.

Totals

The total of transfer payments and schooling costs is the appropriate measure of government expenditures to use in an assessment of the costs and benefits of immigration. The graph shows that the per capita total expenditures on natives are much greater than the per capita expenditures on immigrants—roughly $3,800 vs. $2,200 or $2,600.

It is quite astonishing that the estimates for natives are so much higher than those for immigrants. The gap derives mainly from the costs for the elderly. Of course these estimates are very messy because of the age composition of the immigrant population—many of whom came in recent years—and other uncertainties in the estimates.

But one can draw two conclusions with great surety:

1) The slightly greater expenditures for immigrants on the narrowly defined welfare programs are more than offset by other categories. Indeed, they are dwarfed by them; therefore, the welfare programs alone deserve little attention. 2) Overall expenditures for natives are much greater than those for immigrants.

"Congress no longer can afford to ignore the growing scourge of corporate welfare."

Corporate Welfare Should Be Abolished

Stephen Moore and Dean Stansel

"Corporate welfare"—subsidies and tax breaks intended to protect particular industries—is estimated to cost the federal government billions of dollars in direct spending and billions more in foregone tax revenue. In the following viewpoint, Stephen Moore and Dean Stansel argue that corporate welfare not only wastes taxpayers' money but also hurts consumers through higher prices and even harms the industries it is intended to protect by distorting market forces. Business subsidies should be abolished immediately, they assert. Moore is director of fiscal policy analysis and Stansel is a fiscal policy analyst at the Cato Institute, a conservative libertarian think tank in Washington, D.C.

As you read, consider the following questions:

1. What is the yearly cost to taxpayers of business subsidies, according to Moore and Stansel?
2. What is the yearly cost to consumers of trade restrictions, in the authors' estimation?
3. According to the Progressive Policy Institute, quoted by the authors, how much tax money does the federal government lose by giving tax benefits to particular industries?

Secretary of Labor Robert Reich was right on target late in 1994 when he identified "Federal aid to dependent corporations" as a major contributor to the budget crisis. He also was correct to challenge Congressional Republicans and Washington think tanks to propose termination of Federal activities that fall into the category of "corporate welfare."

The list of corporate subsidy programs is longer and the dollar expenditures are far greater than most members of Congress and the Clinton Administration suspect. Corporate pork is pervasive. For instance, Congress funds more than 125 programs that subsidize private businesses. Subsidy programs to such businesses cost Federal taxpayers more than $85,000,000,000 annually, and the dollar amount has been growing substantially in recent years. Every major Cabinet department has become a conduit for government funding on private industry. Within some Cabinet agencies, such as the Departments of Agriculture and Commerce, almost every spending program underwrites private businesses. . . .

Congress no longer can afford to ignore the growing scourge of corporate welfare. Any serious attempt to balance the budget will require a strategy for getting businesses off the $85,000,000,000 annual dole.

Countering the Arguments for Subsidies

The Clinton Administration and other proponents of Federal subsidies to the private sector often maintain government support of American business is in the national interest. A multitude of economic, national security, and social arguments are voiced to justify corporate aid. Government support is said to protect industries from failure to preserve high-paying American jobs; subsidize research activities that private industries would not finance themselves; counteract the business subsidies of foreign governments to ensure a "level playing field"; boost high-technology companies whose profitability is vital to American economic success in the twenty-first century; maintain the viability of "strategic industries" that are essential to national security; finance ventures that otherwise would be considered too risky for private capital markets; and assist socially disadvantaged groups, such as minorities and women, to establish new businesses.

On the surface, that kind of policy may seem to promote America's economic interest. However, there are at least eight reasons such policies are misguided and dangerous.

The Federal government has a disappointing record of picking industrial winners and losers. The function of private capital markets is to direct billions of dollars of capital to industries and firms that offer the highest potential rate of return. The capital markets, in effect, are in the business of selecting corporate winners and losers. The underlying premise of Federal business subsidies is that the government can direct the limited pool of capital funds more effectively than venture capitalists and private money managers can. Decades of experience, though, prove that government agencies have a much less successful track record than private money managers of correctly selecting winners. The average delinquency rate is higher for government loan programs (eight percent) than for commercial lenders (three percent). The Small Business Administration delinquency rates reached over 20 percent in the early and mid-1980s; the Farmers Home Administration delinquency rate has approached 50 percent.

A Waste of Money

Corporate welfare is a huge drain on the Federal treasury for little economic benefit. It is supposed to offer a positive long-term economic return for taxpayers, but the evidence shows that government "investments" have a low or negative rate of return. In the late 1960s, the Federal government spent nearly $1,000,000,000 on the Supersonic Transport, which experts in Washington expected would revolutionize air travel. Instead, the project went bankrupt and never flew a single passenger. In the late 1970s, the Federal government expended more than $2,000,000,000 of taxpayer money on the Synthetic Fuels Corporation—a public-private project that Department of Energy officials thought would provide new sources of energy for America. The SFC was closed down in the 1980s, never having produced a single kilowatt of electricity.

Corporate welfare creates an uneven playing field. Business subsidies—often said to be justified because they correct distortions in the marketplace—create huge market distortions of their own. The major effect of corporate subsidies is to divert credit and capital to politically well-connected firms at the expense of their politically less influential competitors. Sematech, for example, was launched to promote the U.S. microchip industry over rivals in Japan and Germany. In practice, it has become a cartel of the large U.S. chip producers—such as Intel—that unfairly handicaps the hundreds of smaller American producers. Farm subsidies create another arbitrary distortion. Agricultural price supports are alleged to be critical to the survival of American farmers. The truth is that, of the 400 classified farm commodities, about two dozen receive more than 90 percent of the assistance funds. Over 80 percent of the subsidies enrich farmers with a net worth of more than $500,000.

Corporate welfare fosters an incestuous relationship between government and business. Government and politics are inseparable. Much of what passes today as benign industrial policy is little more than a political payoff to favored industries or businesses. Taxpayer dollars that are used to subsidize private firms routinely are returned to Washington in the form of political contributions and lobbying activities to secure even more tax dollars. For instance, the outdated Rural Electrification Administration survives primarily because of the lobbying efforts of the National Rural Electrical Cooperative Association in America. With a $78,000,000 budget, that association is one of the most influential and heavily financed lobbying groups in Washington.

Politically Motivated Spending

During the 1992 presidential campaign, Vice President Dan Quayle traveled to Michigan to announce a $250,000,000 plan to upgrade the M-1 tank. It just happened to be built by General Dynamics in Sterling Heights, Michigan. Before the campaign, the Bush Administration had argued convincingly that, in the post–Cold War era, the more expensive tank was unnecessary.

Go After Corporate Welfare

Republicans have already declared war on Aid to Families with Dependent Children and other forms of welfare—including food stamps, housing assistance and child nutrition—that cost about $50 billion a year. Secretary of Labor Robert Reich challenges them to go after another form of welfare, equally large or larger, which he mockingly labels "Aid to Dependent Corporations." Corporate welfare, according to a meticulous though partial list drawn up by the Democratic Leadership Council, exceeds $40 billion a year. The Leadership Council estimates that a thorough search would turn up between $60 billion and $75 billion a year.

New York Times, January 17, 1995.

Many of the top recipients of technology research grants awarded by the Clinton Administration were substantial contributors to the Clinton campaign or the Democratic National Committee. For example, eight Fortune 500 firms that were multi-million-dollar award-winners of the Advanced Technology Program or the Technology Reinvestment Project in 1994 also were large Democratic campaign contributors, according to Federal Election Commission data compiled by Common Cause. These included AT&T, Boeing, Chevron, General Electric, McDonnell Douglas, Shell, Texaco, and United Technology. At the very least, such golden handshake programs create an impression that government is for sale.

Corporate welfare is anti-consumer. One of the main effects of many corporate subsidy programs is to raise costs to consumers. Trade restrictions, often sought by politically powerful industries, are estimated to cost consumers $80,000,000,000 a year. The sugar program is estimated to cost consumers several billion dollars a year, according to a U.S. Department of Commerce study that concluded: "Because sugar is an ingredient in many food items, the effect of the sugar program is similar to a regressive sales tax, which hits lower-income families harder than upper-income families."

The most efficient way to promote business in America is to reduce the overall cost and regulatory burden of government. Corporate welfare is predicated on the misguided notion that the best way to enhance business profitability in America is to do so one firm at a time. A much more effective way to boost the competitiveness and productivity of American industry is to create a level playing field, thus minimizing government interference in the marketplace and substantially reducing tax rates and regulatory burdens. For example, all the Federal government's efforts to promote the big three U.S. automobile companies are insignificant compared with the regulatory burden on that industry, which now adds an estimated $3,000 to the sticker price of a new car. Eliminating just half the business subsidies in the Federal budget would generate enough savings to pay for the entire elimination of the capital gains tax. Clearly, a zero capital gains tax would generate far more jobs and business start-ups than the scores of targeted business handouts in the Federal budget.

Subsidies Destroy Market Forces

Corporate welfare is anti-capitalist. It converts the American businessman from a capitalist into a lobbyist. Corporate welfare, notes Wall Street financier Theodore J. Forstmann, has led to the creation of the "statist businessman in America." The statist businessman is "a conservator, not a creator; a caretaker, not a risk taker, an argument against capitalism even though he is not a capitalist at all." For instance, the Fanjul family, owner of several large sugar farms in the Florida Everglades, earns an estimated $60,000,000 a year in artificial profits thanks to price supports and import quotas. The Fanjul family is a fierce defender of the sugar program and, in 1992, contributed $350,000 to political campaigns. All of that has a corrosive effect on the American free enterprise system.

Corporate welfare is unconstitutional. The most critical reason government should end corporate subsidy programs is that they lie outside Congress' limited spending authority under the Constitution. Nowhere in the Constitution is Congress granted the authority to spend funds to subsidize the computer industry, enter into joint ventures with automobile companies, or guarantee

144

loans to favored business owners.

Government provides special benefits to individual industries and companies through a vast array of policy levers. The three major business benefits come in the forms of special tax breaks, trade policies, and spending programs.

When Reich protested against "aid to dependent corporations," his criticism was directed toward "special tax benefits for particular industries." The Democratic Leadership Council's Progressive Policy Institute has specified some thirty such "tax subsidies" that led to a loss of $134,000,000,000 in Federal revenues over five years. . . .

Abolish All Subsidies

There are at least 125 separate programs providing subsidies to particular industries and firms with a price tag exceeding $85,000,000,000 per year. We recommend the immediate abolition of all such programs.

Because they intermingle government dollars with corporate political clout, business subsidies have a corrupting influence on America's system of democratic government and entrepreneurial capitalism. Despite the conventional orthodoxy in Washington that the nation needs an even closer alliance between business and politics, the truth is that both government and the marketplace would work better if they kept a healthy distance from each other.

It is ironic that at a time when the Federal government is in litigation with Microsoft, perhaps America's most innovative and profitable high-technology corporation in decades, for successfully dominating the software industry, Congress is spending hundreds of millions of dollars trying to prop up the firm's less efficient computer industry rivals. A situation exists whereby Federal regulatory policies increasingly are geared toward punishing success, while Federal corporate welfare policies increasingly reward failure. That is not the way to preserve America's industrial might.

"What ['corporate welfare' cutters] would really be doing is increasing taxes on the nation's business owners, workers, and consumers."

Corporate Subsidies Are Beneficial

Rob Norton

Conservatives and liberals who want to reduce government spending advocate cutting "corporate welfare"—subsidies and tax breaks intended to stimulate certain industries. In the following viewpoint, Rob Norton argues that although some outdated business subsidies could be cut, many others help U.S. industries to remain competitive in world markets. Furthermore, he contends, cutting corporations' legitimate tax breaks would simply result in higher prices to consumers. Norton is assistant managing editor of *Fortune* magazine.

As you read, consider the following questions:

1. What corporate subsidies does Norton cite as examples of traditional industry supports?
2. What example does the author give of a price support that deserves the "welfare" label?
3. According to the author, what would happen if corporations had fewer tax deductions?

Expect to hear the phrase "corporate welfare" a lot as the 1995 battle over the federal budget escalates. "Corporate welfare" is the fiscal catch phrase du jour—shorthand for all the federal spending and tax measures that benefit the business community. The Democratic minority is insisting that the corporate side of the budget be attacked just as vigorously as the social spending programs the Republicans are gunning for. Even some Republicans, like House Budget Committee Chairman John Kasich, have come up with lists of eminently dispensable business subsidies. Every think tank along the Potomac—from the libertarian Cato Institute to Ralph Nader's leftish Center for Study of Responsive Law—has its "corporate welfare" hit list.

What Is "Corporate Welfare"?

"Corporate welfare" is a brilliantly conceived phrase. It evokes all the pejorative stereotypes that have grown up around social-welfare spending in America: the suspicion that many recipients are undeserving, the conviction that honest work is being discouraged, the overall odor of bureaucracy and inefficiency.

But what exactly do the politicos mean when they say "corporate welfare"? First come the direct government subsidies to corporations. These include the traditional support for energy and mining and historical curiosities such as the Rural Electrification Administration, as well as more recent subsidies designed to help U.S. industry become more competitive—like the $90 million per year that flows to the nation's computer makers through Sematech. Robert J. Shapiro of the Progressive Policy Institute—a centrist Democratic think tank—catalogues 89 spending programs that could be cut for budget savings of $131 billion over five years. Far more sweeping is the Cato Institute's list, which targets 127 programs, worth $86 billion per year.

Deciding Which Subsidies to Cut

Many—probably most—of these subsidies deserve to die. Would-be budget reformers and true fiscal conservatives have been stalking them for decades. But what makes them "corporate welfare" instead of merely unwise federal spending? To decide that, here are four questions that should be asked of any program financed by Washington: Does it make sense on its merits? Is it something that government can clearly do better than the private sector? Is it important enough to shoulder aside other national needs in an age of fiscal restraint? And is it efficiently run? If the answer is no to one or more, the program should be eliminated, cut, or reformed. If it fails this test and at the same time is fattening someone's corporate oxen, then it deserves the "welfare" label. Agricultural price supports are a good example: Consumers pay out $1.4 billion per year because of sugar price supports, with an estimated 40 percent going to the richest 1 percent of sugar farmers.

"Corporate welfare" is an even more slippery concept when applied to tax benefits. At first this idea sounds plausible. If the law lets companies escape tax liabilities via deductions that don't seem to serve the public interest—the three-martini lunch is the classic case—isn't that a giveaway, just as though the Treasury sent out checks? Short answer: not really.

Don't Confuse Tax Breaks with Subsidies

Critics of "corporate welfare" assume that the government is entitled to a certain percentage of corporate profits and that any company that pays less is being unjustly enriched. They even have a name for this concept in the nation's capital. They call it a "tax expenditure." One example: Companies are allowed to deduct advertising costs instead of depreciating them. If they couldn't, the government might collect some $18 billion more in taxes over the next five years.

The fallacy in this line of thinking is that current tax rates are not fixed by natural law. They are products of the same political process that decided what kinds of income should be taxed. If corporations had fewer deductions, tax rates would be lower. To talk about legitimate deductions as though they were subsidies to corporations is naive.

Business Subsidies Support Jobs

U.S. Commerce Department officials argue that if the government's business promotion programs are put into the "corporate welfare" waste bin, the budget cutters will actually hurt, not help the economy. . . .

According to the department's calculations, the $269 million it has spent on export advocacy in the past year has helped push $20 billion worth of exports out the door and support some 300,000 jobs.

Amy Kaslow, *Christian Science Monitor*, June 16, 1995.

An even more basic problem with the tax side of "corporate welfare" arises if you consider a question rarely asked in Washington: Who really pays the corporate income tax? Corporations, of course, ultimately can't pay taxes—only people can. Most economists understand this, and there's a whole subspecialty in public-finance economics that deals with the "incidence" of taxes—who it is that ultimately bears their burden.

For the corporate income tax, the pain falls on stockholders, employees, and customers, but there's no precise way to measure how it gets apportioned.

So the "corporate welfare" brigade can squawk all they want about ending "aid to dependent corporations" by closing tax loopholes and forcing fat-cat companies to "pay their fair share." But what they would really be doing is increasing taxes on the nation's business owners, workers, and consumers in ways that are indirect, difficult to observe, and impossible to measure.

Periodical Bibliography

The following articles have been selected to supplement the diverse views presented in this chapter. Addresses are provided for periodicals not indexed in the *Readers' Guide to Periodical Literature*, the *Alternative Press Index*, or the *Social Sciences Index*.

Eric Alterman	"The Reich Stuff," *Mother Jones*, July/August 1995.
Brian Doherty	"Big Daddy," *Reason*, June 1996.
Nicholas Eberstadt	"Prosperous Paupers and Affluent Savages," *Society*, January/February 1996.
Howard Gleckman	"Welfare Cuts: Now, It's Corporate America's Turn," *Business Week*, April 10, 1995.
Linda Grant	"Getting Business Off the Dole," *U.S. News & World Report*, April 10, 1995.
Rick Henderson	"Fact and Friction," *Reason*, February 1995.
Martin Kramer	"The Myth About Welfare Moms," *Time*, July 3, 1995.
Mike Males	"In Defense of Teenaged Mothers," *Progressive*, August 1994.
Stephen Moore	"Mr. Corporate Welfare," *National Review*, January 29, 1996.
Paul Offner	"Welfare Dads," *New Republic*, February 13, 1995.
Katha Pollitt	"Devil Women," *New Yorker*, February 26–March 4, 1996.
Katha Pollitt	"Subject to Debate," *Nation*, January 30, 1995.
Jay Rosen	"The War on Immigrants: Why the Courts Can't Save Us," *New Republic*, January 30, 1995.
Jennifer Wolff	"The Real Faces of Welfare," *Glamour*, September 1995.

4 CHAPTER

How Should the Welfare System Be Reformed?

WELFARE

Chapter Preface

With his 1992 promise to "end welfare as we know it," President Bill Clinton initiated a national debate on welfare reform. The plethora of proposed reforms have focused mainly on cost-saving measures designed to move recipients off the welfare rolls and into jobs. But alongside the wrangling over how to save money has been a debate over who is best able to carry out the reform proposals: the states or the federal government.

The governors of many states have proposed eliminating federal welfare program requirements and allowing the states to run individually designed programs. Advocates of this plan argue that federal programs, with one-size-fits-all requirements, have created or exacerbated problems such as out-of-wedlock births and welfare dependency. States are closer to the people involved in the system, they contend, and therefore are better able to identify and solve such problems. William F. Weld, the Republican governor of Massachusetts and an advocate of welfare reform in his state, asserts, "If the federal government would just release us from its bureaucracy and nonsense, we'd make these programs better for those they serve, and we'd do it for less money."

Opponents of the plan to turn welfare over to the states maintain that federal control of the welfare system is necessary to guarantee that needy people receive aid. If the federal government does not mandate spending levels and provide the revenue to meet those levels, these opponents contend, states may be forced to cut levels of aid or to eliminate welfare programs altogether in order to save money. Without federal program guidelines, asserts Betty Reid Mandell, professor emeritus of sociology at Bridgewater State College in Massachusetts, "people who play by the rules, whatever they may be, will be denied benefits arbitrarily . . . when a fiscal crisis occurs" in their state.

Saving money is only one of the goals of welfare reform. Other frequently mentioned objectives include discouraging illegitimate births, particularly among teenaged girls, and ending welfare dependency. The viewpoints in the following chapter debate the effectiveness of various proposed reforms.

"Training and work mandates should be used as tools to discourage out-of-wedlock births."

Welfare Reform Should Discourage Illegitimate Births

Douglas J. Besharov

Both Democratic and Republican welfare reform plans include proposals for work training incentives to encourage personal responsibility among welfare recipients. In the following viewpoint, Douglas J. Besharov contends that job training and public service jobs are the best tools for reducing welfare dependency among poor single (and especially teenaged) mothers. If these women were provided with opportunities more rewarding than those currently offered by welfare, the author argues, they would view having out-of-wedlock children as an inconvenience and would be dissuaded from having such children. Besharov is a scholar at the American Enterprise Institute, a conservative think tank in Washington, D.C.

As you read, consider the following questions:

1. How many years do unwed mothers spend on welfare, according to Besharov?
2. According to the author, why do most welfare mothers stay on welfare even when they are forced to work?
3. According to Joycelyn Elders, cited by the author, what percentage of teen mothers say their pregnancies were intended?

Douglas J. Besharov, "Working to Make Welfare a Chore," *Wall Street Journal*, February 9, 1994. Reprinted by permission of the author.

The nation is in the midst of yet another effort to reform the welfare system. But this time, after thirty years of denial, almost everyone now agrees that real reform requires doing something about out-of-wedlock births, especially among teenagers. And, for a change, there might be real money to spend. Both Democrats and Republicans are talking about $6 billion to $10 billion a year for a welfare reform program, even under today's tight budget constraints.

Unfortunately, though, the president's welfare planners are seeking to use job training and public service jobs to make poorly educated unwed mothers self-sufficient, which won't work. Instead, training and work mandates should be used as tools to discourage out-of-wedlock births in the first place.

The problem has grown too large to ignore, as Charles Murray and others have noted. In 1991, about 30 percent of American births were out of wedlock, reflecting a steady increase from 1960, when this figure was only 5 percent. Unwed mothers now head half the families on welfare, double the proportion in 1970. They average almost ten years on welfare, twice as long as divorced mothers, thus swelling the ranks of long-term welfare dependents.

Job Training Will Not Reduce Welfare Rolls

What to do? President Clinton would give all recipients up to two years of job training and education. But even the best job training programs have had little success in reducing welfare rolls. Five percent reductions—not nearly enough to "end welfare as we know it," Bill Clinton's much-repeated campaign pledge—are considered major accomplishments.

This is why Mr. Clinton also proposes to time-limit welfare benefits. He says that if, after two years, a welfare mother does not get a job, she should be placed in a public service job. The job is supposed to give her work experience and to serve as an incentive to get off welfare, since she will have to work anyway.

The evidence, however, suggests that work requirements do not reduce caseloads, at least not immediately. The Manpower Demonstration Research Corp. (MDRC) recently reviewed the mandatory work programs in West Virginia; Cook County, Illinois; and in two sites in San Diego, California. In no site did the work requirement reduce welfare payments.

Why do most single mothers stay on welfare, even after they are forced to work for their benefits? Their "welfare jobs" may be better than anything they can get in the real world of work; they are probably less demanding than actual jobs; and there is little chance of being laid off or fired. Moreover, especially in areas of high unemployment, there may be no other jobs available for poorly educated women with little work experience.

Recognizing these realities, and to save money, the president's welfare reform working group is now suggesting that Mr. Clinton's proposed public service requirement be watered down. This would be a mistake. In fact, work requirements should be applied much earlier in the welfare careers of young, unwed mothers.

Illegitimacy and Welfare Reform

Illegitimacy and its attendant social pathologies are among the most serious threats to American society, and welfare is illegitimacy's economic lifeline. Addressing out of wedlock births is increasingly recognized as the sine qua non of real welfare reform.

William Bennett, Jack Kemp, and Vin Weber, *Washington Times*, April 24, 1994.

Surgeon General Joycelyn Elders often cites a 1988 survey in which 87 percent of unwed teen mothers said that their babies' births were "intended." But this includes 63 percent who said that the birth was "mistimed." And when clinicians ask the more telling question, whether having a baby would disrupt their lives—that is, whether it would be inconvenient—few say "yes." For example, in 1990, Laurie Zabin of the Johns Hopkins School of Public Health and Hygiene surveyed pregnant, inner-city black teens; only 31 percent said that they "believed a baby would present a problem." Making illegitimacy more inconvenient, what economists would call raising its opportunity cost, is the key to reducing out-of-wedlock births.

Education and Work Will Discourage Teen Births

Increasing the life prospects of disadvantaged teens is surely the best way to raise the opportunity costs of having a baby out of wedlock. A good education and real job opportunities are the best contraceptives. Nevertheless, different welfare policies could have a real impact. The ultimate "inconvenience," of course, would be to deny welfare benefits altogether. But there is a less drastic way: Impose an unequivocal requirement to finish high school and then to work.

From almost the first day that a young, unwed mother goes on welfare, she should be engaged in mandatory skill-building activities. The first priority should be that she finish high school, or at least demonstrate basic proficiency in math and reading. After that, if she is unable to find work, she should be assigned to a public service job, as the president promised.

The political pressure from unions, especially, will be for these

155

public service positions to be "real jobs" at "decent wages." This would raise costs to prohibitive levels and make recipients even less likely to leave the rolls. Instead, the focus should be on activities that are appropriate for inexperienced young women.

Examples of such activities were described by MDRC's Thomas Brock, who studied the four mandatory work programs mentioned above as well as six others. The activities "did not teach new skills, but neither were they 'make work.' Most were entry-level clerical positions or janitorial/maintenance jobs," such as office aides and receptionists for a community nonprofit agency, mail clerks for city agencies, assistants in day-care programs for children or handicapped adults, helpers in public works departments sweeping and repairing streets, and gardening in city parks. And, although the work requirement did not immediately reduce caseloads, the value of the services rendered together with other savings exceeded the program's cost to taxpayers in three of the four sites.

Despite the real value of the services provided, such a program would be very expensive. But because of its prophylactic purpose, the work requirement could be applied to new applicants only. The long phase-in period would sharply lower initial costs—and allow modifications in program rules and administration based on what is learned during the first stages of implementation.

One hopes that such activities raise the skills and, therefore, the employability of current recipients. The fundamental purpose of mandated work, however, should be to raise the inconvenience level of being on welfare by requiring these young women to be someplace—doing something constructive—every day. The object would be to discourage their younger sisters and friends from thinking that a life on welfare is an attractive option. Strengthened child-support enforcement would increase the inconvenience level for their boyfriends who got them pregnant, but describing how to achieve that end is a complicated subject for another day.

"Welfare reform has turned into a mean-spirited campaign to modify women's behavior and dismantle the welfare state."

Welfare Reform Should Not Punish Women for Having Children

Mimi Abramovitz

Welfare reform proposals have focused on encouraging welfare recipients to work and discouraging them from having additional children. In the following viewpoint, Mimi Abramovitz argues that such proposals unfairly punish poor women for exercising their reproductive rights and choosing to be mothers. She maintains that existing workfare programs have not been effective and have simply prevented welfare recipients from being able to care for the children full-time. Abramovitz is a professor of social policy at Hunter College of Social Work in New York City and is the author of *Regulating the Lives of Women: Social Welfare Policy from Colonial Times to the Present*.

As you read, consider the following questions:

1. In Abramovitz's opinion, what was Congress's original intention when it created Aid to Families with Dependent Children?
2. What percentage of welfare families have one child, and what percentage have two children, according to the author?
3. According to the author, what percentage of welfare households are headed by teen mothers?

Adapted and reprinted by permission of Mimi Abramovitz from her paper "Welfare and Women's Lives: Toward a Feminist Understanding of the Reform Debate," presented at Women for Women: Against the Contract, City University of New York, March 8, 1995.

Frances Fox Piven wrote in the summer of 1994 about the faulty assumptions and cruel logic of the Clinton administration's welfare reform proposals. No one could have guessed then just how far and how fast the public debate on welfare would swing to the right. As I write today (in mid-April 1995), the Republicans' "Personal Responsibility Act," which is even more punitive than Clinton's "Work and Personal Responsibility Act," has passed the House and awaits consideration in the Senate. Even if Clinton vetoes this first bill [he vetoed it in January 1996], it's almost certain that some kind of regressive welfare "reform" will become law before the 1996 elections. Welfare reform is bad for women, because they are the direct target of a drive to modify women's behavior; bad for children, who will see less of their mothers; bad for labor, who will face more competition for fewer jobs; bad for the poor, because it makes them poorer; and bad for the middle class, because their programs are next.

So we on the left have our work cut out for us. Just as the right patiently laid the groundwork over twenty years for its assault on the public sector, we need to do the slow work of building cohesive movements for social justice. A crucial part of this work will be raising public consciousness of welfare as a feminist issue—not just in the superficial sense that most welfare recipients are women, but also with the understanding that the availability of welfare affects *all* women's ability to resist sexist workplaces and family structures.

Welfare Reform Is an Attack on Women

Welfare reform has turned into a mean-spirited campaign to modify women's behavior and dismantle the welfare state. When Aid to Families with Dependent Children (AFDC) was created in 1935, Congress's intention was to cushion poverty and to enable mothers to stay home with their kids. AFDC has never performed either of these functions well, and feminists and the left have criticized it for years.

But now things have gone from bad to worse. Instead of fixing AFDC to compensate for the falling standard of living, the new welfare reform deflects attention from the sagging economy by maligning the marital, childbearing, and parenting behavior of poor women. To build support for their plans, the welfare cutters evoke false stereotypes of recipients as culturally adrift welfare queens who prefer welfare to work, live high on the hog, cheat the government, and have kids for money. The rhetoric of this assault is highly racialized. Although 40 percent of the welfare caseload nationwide is white, the reformers do not hesitate to pander to white voters' worst instincts. Richard Nixon had his "southern strategy," Ronald Reagan had his welfare queen,

George Bush had Willie Horton, and today's politicians have welfare reform.

Women Want to Work

The first target of welfare reform is women's work behavior. Time limits and workfare plans presume that women do not want to work and need to be coerced into the labor market. But in fact, 70 percent of all AFDC recipients do leave the rolls within two years for work or marriage. A significant number of these women return within five years because of unstable jobs, failed relationships, or the lack of child care and health benefits. The remaining 30 percent are people who cannot compete effectively in today's labor market because of lack of education and skills, illness, disability, or emotional problems. They need supportive services, not punitive reforms.

The push for mandatory work requirements also ignores years of research showing that welfare-to-work programs have only modest results. This is not terribly surprising. First, there are not enough jobs for all those willing and able to work—and the Federal Reserve works hard to keep things that way. Second, the low-paying, part-time jobs available to poor women lack benefits and union protection. Given these conditions, the administration's promise "to make work pay for those who try hard and play by the rules" rings hollow for welfare mothers. It also devalues their work at home. Finally, cutting welfare means the loss of many public sector jobs, which for years have provided large numbers of white women and women of color a way out of poverty.

The second target of welfare reform, women's childbearing behavior, challenges women's reproductive rights. Both parties have expanded the child exclusion provision, which denies aid to children born on AFDC, and stiffened paternity procedures. These changes imply that women on welfare have large families, when in fact the average family on welfare is a mother and two children, the same as the rest of us. Forty-three percent of AFDC families have one child and 30 percent have two. Since you have to have at least one child to qualify for AFDC, this means that most women have just one additional child while on the rolls. It also suggests that women on welfare do have children for money. But seventy-six researchers recently announced that there is no evidence for a link between the availability of welfare and a woman's childbearing decisions.

The Republicans have made controlling women's reproductive choices the main goal of welfare reform. The stated purpose of their bill is to put an end to "illegitimacy." They say mother-only families—encouraged by welfare—have produced drug dealers, drive-by shooters, and the deficit. To end "illegitimacy," they plan a range of horrific child exclusion provisions, some denying aid to children and young unwed mothers forever. The Republican paternity procedures hold back AFDC until the state establishes paternity, which can take months, leaving even more women out in the cold. If the pregnancies persist despite these penalties, the Republicans tell mothers to turn to relatives, apply for private charity, or place their children in "orphanages."

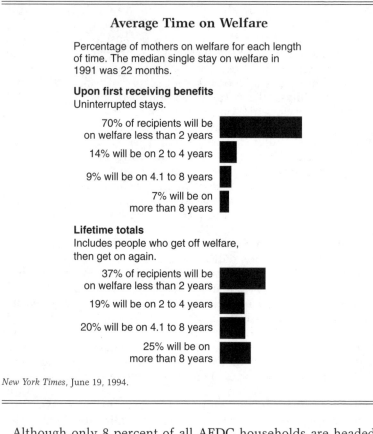

Average Time on Welfare

Percentage of mothers on welfare for each length of time. The median single stay on welfare in 1991 was 22 months.

Upon first receiving benefits
Uninterrupted stays.

70% of recipients will be on welfare less than 2 years

14% will be on 2 to 4 years

9% will be on 4.1 to 8 years

7% will be on more than 8 years

Lifetime totals
Includes people who get off welfare, then get on again.

37% of recipients will be on welfare less than 2 years

19% will be on 2 to 4 years

20% will be on 4.1 to 8 years

25% will be on more than 8 years

New York Times, June 19, 1994.

Although only 8 percent of all AFDC households are headed by teens, the welfare reformers pander to public worries about "babies having babies." If preventing teen pregnancy were the real goal of welfare reform, we would hear more about sex education, family planning, abortion services, and awareness of the complexities of teen pregnancy.

Attacks on Responsible Parents

The third target of welfare reform is the parenting behavior of poor women and men. The welfare reform debate displays a deep distrust of parenting by poor women. Supporters of "orphanages" publicly suggest that any caretaking is better than that provided by welfare mothers, even though many have hired poor women in their own homes.

In the name of promoting parental responsibility, welfare reform forces single mothers to work, shrinks the AFDC check, and otherwise undercuts the conditions for effective parenting. Forcing women to work makes it harder for mothers to supervise their children. This makes little sense, especially in neighborhoods plagued by poor schools, lack of health care, substandard housing and in some cases drugs, crime, and violence. Stricter child support enforcement clamps down on the parenting behavior of so-called "deadbeat dads." While men should be expected to support their children, welfare reform ignores that most welfare fathers are poor and unemployed, that some are already involved with their children, and that an aggressive pursuit of child support could subject women to male violence. All these efforts to enforce responsible parenting defy the research that shows that the deprivations of poverty, not the receipt of a welfare check, impair children's development on all fronts. Although the combined value of AFDC and food stamps falls below the poverty line in all fifty states, the welfare reformers are silent on raising the grant and ending poverty as we know it.

The current attack harms poor women and their children first and foremost for being poor. But welfare reform also fits into a broader strategy designed to take back the gains made by *all* women during the past thirty years. The proposed changes attack the rights of all women to decent pay, to control their own sexuality, to establish families free of abusive relationships, and to survive outside of the rigid family forms endorsed by the religious right. They do this by undercutting women's economic independence, weakening their caretaking supports, and threatening their reproductive rights.

Welfare Is a Woman's Issue

Cutting AFDC benefits undercuts all women's economic independence by depriving women of a small but critical alternative to male and market income. Without this backup many women facing hard times will have more trouble resisting an exploitative job, escaping an abusive relationship, or simply deciding to raise children alone. By forcing women to work, welfare reform twists the gains of the women's movement against poor women. Feminism has called for more choices, greater opportunities, and well-paying work for women—not coercion, workfare, and poverty-level jobs.

Welfare reform threatens the rights of all women by shifting the costs of caretaking back to the home. The attack on welfare fuels a larger attack on the nation's health, education, child care, income support, and social service programs which among other things have underwritten the cost of family maintenance and eased the caretaking burdens of middle-class as well as poor women.

Welfare reform also threatens the reproductive rights of every woman. Efforts to penalize non-marital births are not far removed from the anti-abortion movement's challenge to women's reproductive choices. The foes of abortion have not yet won their battle in full. But if the government wins the right to control the bodies of poor women on welfare, it will be much easier to control the bodies of all women.

Welfare is an issue for women because politicians have built support for their attack on women's rights by blaming all women for the nation's woes. Women, welfare, and now affirmative action are being scapegoated to ease the moral panic generated by new family structures and greater economic independence among women. Welfare reform enforces traditional work and family forms by disciplining those defined as "not playing by the rules." The reformers openly hope that their stiff penalties will send a message to women about what happens to those who do not marry, who raise kids on their own, and otherwise step out of role. Since any woman can be tarred and feathered in this way, we must ask: Who made the rules? Who benefits from the rules? And can single mothers even play by a set of rules that defines their family structure as out of bounds?

While the Democrats' "Work and Personal Responsibility Act" bids for conservative votes by making welfare leaner and meaner, the Republican "Personal Responsibility Act" ups the ante by ending the welfare state altogether. It cuts welfare grants, converts major income support programs into state-administered block grants, and wipes out the federal guarantee of funds for all those who apply for aid. Without the federal backup, fiscally strapped states will not be able to serve all those in need when the population grows or the economy sinks. You'd never guess from all the fuss that the $24 billion spent on AFDC benefits in 1994 represented only 1 percent of the federal budget—4 percent when Medicaid and food stamps are included.

Despite all this, I can end on an optimistic note. Poor and middle-class women are not taking the blame, the punishment, or the coercion lying down. Since 1987, poor women have been fighting the war on the poor through such groups as the National Welfare Rights Union. This time around, they have been joined by large numbers of welfare advocates who are also working to limit punitive policies and to secure "real" welfare reform. Reversing past practice, these activists are spanning the traditional schisms between welfare recipients, feminist activists, and human service workers. The infrastructure built up during the past ten years of fighting right-wing social policies was mobilized on Valentine's Day 1995, when organizations in thirty-eight states and seventy-seven cities from Maine to Hawaii participated in a national day of action to stop the war on the poor. This growing network is now well-positioned to be mobilized again, and again, and again.

These grassroots actions are critical. The historical record shows that the powers that be rarely act and social change rarely occurs for the better unless pressured from below. Unless today's politicians know that we mean business, they will not budge.

"'Welfare-to-work' mandates are intended to speed the transition to work and to signal that welfare is not a 'free ride.'"

Welfare Recipients Should Be Trained and Required to Work

Judith M. Gueron

Since the early 1970s, welfare programs have promoted job training for aid recipients. In the following viewpoint, Judith M. Gueron points out that "welfare-to-work" programs have produced some successful results. Job training programs can work, she maintains, if sufficient funds are provided to ensure success and if enough public service jobs are created to absorb welfare recipients who cannot find work in the private sector. Gueron is president of Manpower Demonstration Research Corporation (MDRC), a nonpartisan organization that studies welfare issues.

As you read, consider the following questions:

1. What are the lessons learned from programs in the 1980s, as listed by Gueron?
2. What is the negative side of mandatory community service work programs, in the author's opinion?
3. According to the author, why are some people unable to work?

Judith M. Gueron, "The Route to Welfare Reform," *Brookings Review*, Summer 1994. Reprinted by permission of the Brookings Institution Press.

The federal cash welfare program—Aid to Families with Dependent Children—was created in 1935 to help children. The object was to reduce poverty without forcing mothers, primarily widows, into the labor force. Since then, numerous changes in the social landscape—women pouring into the labor market, the increasing cost of welfare, the growing number of single-parent families headed by unwed mothers, and concern about long-term reliance on welfare—have undermined the 1930s view that welfare should provide an alternative to work. The focus of AFDC has shifted from reducing poverty to reducing dependency, with welfare recast as a temporary way station on the route to work.

Since 1967 the primary thrust of reform has been making welfare less of an entitlement (if you were poor, you got money) and more of a reciprocal obligation. The theory seems simple. Welfare recipients have to look for and accept a job or participate in work-related activities such as education, work experience, or vocational skills training. If not, they risk losing benefits. In turn, the government has to provide employment-related services and supports. These "welfare-to-work" mandates are intended to speed the transition to work and to signal that welfare is not a "free ride." They offer people opportunities, but also seek to impose an obligation, using carrots and sticks to change behavior and make welfare less attractive. And they reach many people who might not come forward on their own. But while the principle is simple, reality has proved complex and elusive. A mandate is real only if it offers enough activities to allow all those who are required to participate to do so—and if there are clear consequences (such as benefit cuts) for people who do not.

Since this approach first became law in 1971, grossly inadequate funding has meant that most people have not in fact faced a requirement. Thus the system has been spared a real test of its willingness to sanction nonparticipants.

Finding the Right Balance

Over the years the balance between opportunity and obligation has changed. In the 1970s, after an initial focus on education and training, the emphasis shifted to minimal services directed at quick job placement. During the 1980s, funding was reduced further and the typical state program continued to rely on job search assistance, sometimes also using a newly authorized option to require people to work in exchange for benefits. The Family Support Act of 1988, through its Job Opportunities and Basic Skills Training program (JOBS), sought to strengthen both obligation and opportunity—providing more resources, requiring more people, including teen mothers and others with small children, to participate, and emphasizing education and training.

165

Several unusually rigorous studies of JOBS and pre-JOBS programs show that a variety of approaches were successful in increasing work and reducing welfare costs. Although the results were not dramatic (and many families remained on welfare and in poverty), the programs often saved more than enough to pay back the initial government outlay, an exceptional accomplishment for a government service program. Limited resources usually hampered program operations. But when funding was adequate and management truly committed, welfare-to-work mandates changed the expectations of and opportunities for welfare recipients. Further, results from one of the few states implementing JOBS' school attendance mandate for teen parents have shown that—with a combination of financial incentives, case management, and support services—some young mothers can be encouraged to stay in, or return to, school. Finally, states and localities adopted quite different strategies, and local ownership of program design and goals appeared critical to success.

A Successful Program in California

JOBS' largest measured impacts to date—double-digit increases in the share of AFDC recipients working, a 50 percent increase in average earnings, a one-sixth reduction in welfare payments, impressive effects on long-term recipients—were found in Riverside, California. With adequate funding to reach all mandated participants, the Riverside program communicates high expectations. People understand that they are there for one purpose: to get a job. At orientation, job developers announce job openings; throughout, staff convey a positive message about the value of work and people's potential to succeed. Those in an education program—about half the Riverside participants are— know that if they do not complete it, or at least regularly make progress in it, staff who are closely monitoring their progress will insist that they look for a job.

In Riverside, welfare has changed for everyone in JOBS. But the gap between the exceptional and the average state and local program is wide. The more typical program, while achieving positive results, remains severely strapped for funds, does not reach most of the people who could theoretically be subject to its mandates, and has not dramatically changed the message of welfare.

Challenges in Implementing Time Limits

President Bill Clinton's welfare reform proposal would be another big step in the twenty-five-year effort to convert welfare from an entitlement into a reciprocal obligation. The plan would set a time limit on the opportunity side of JOBS' reciprocal obligation. People could participate in work-promoting services for up to two years. After that, those who could work would have to get an unsubsidized job or, to get continued public support, work in a community service program. In some ways this proposal builds directly on the Family Support Act's vision of parental responsibility and resolves an ambiguity as to when services are to terminate. Surely, at some point, the argument went, the investment in education and training would have to end and people would have to go to work.

The public likes the idea of requiring work after two years of welfare—though, because information about costs is not available, it has not had to consider seriously what it will take to put the idea into action. As Presidents Jimmy Carter and Ronald Reagan found out when they attempted work requirements in somewhat different forms, making this vision work raises tough questions. Can enough "real," rather than make-work, jobs be created? At reasonable cost and without disrupting low-wage labor markets? What will prevent large numbers of women and children from becoming destitute and homeless? How many welfare recipients cannot work? Can and will welfare administrators manage and enforce the new obligations?

The lessons from the 1980s—that well-run programs can modestly reduce, but not eliminate, long-term welfare dependency; that creating many meaningful community service jobs is hard; that monthly participation, at best, will be about 50 percent, with many acceptable reasons for nonparticipation; that adequate resources are key to effective implementation; and that state and local ownership is critical to success—point to five main challenges in implementing time limits.

Beating the Two-Year Time Limit

Time-limiting welfare, with work at the end, will be feasible and affordable only if many more people than is now the case leave AFDC *before* reaching the two-year "cliff," thereby reducing the pressure to create community service positions. With growing evidence that JOBS' insistence on job search, education, or training can speed the transition to work, it is becoming clear that fully implementing JOBS is not an alternative to, but a prerequisite for, any serious discussion of time-limited welfare. The goal of hard-pressed welfare administrators must be to get people off the rolls before they reach the time limit, not to keep them busy in community service jobs afterwards. Making the JOBS services and mandates real for most welfare recipients will require more money to fund and monitor the work-directed activities, federal guidance on successful strategies, and strengthened state and local commitment to operating high-performing programs.

Even if JOBS programs nationwide could match Riverside's success, however, under current rules nearly half of targeted welfare recipients would eventually reach the two-year limit. Some have argued that stepped-up efforts to involve the private sector could greatly reduce this number, but experience suggests clear limits to that approach. Others anticipate that setting a time limit, expanding the earned income tax credit, increasing work incentives within the welfare system, and providing subsidized health coverage and child care for the working poor would encourage many more people to take and keep unsubsidized jobs. These changes should increase the effectiveness of JOBS, but prudence suggests assuming that many welfare recipients will still reach the two-year cliff.

Creating Enough Community Service Jobs

The nation's experience with community service work is limited and mixed. The 1970s Comprehensive Employment and Training Act (CETA) created 750,000 public service jobs, but of uneven quality and amid much controversy. The evidence on requiring welfare recipients to work is more sobering still. Even when political support is enthusiastic—as under Governor Ronald Reagan in California or Mayor Ed Koch in New York City—welfare administrators failed to create many community work experience jobs. (During an average month, New York City had 3,500–4,000 people working, out of an AFDC caseload of about 250,000.) Typical 1980s programs filled fewer than 400 positions, involving only a small percentage of the welfare population and for only short periods. On the positive side, the work was real (if not skill-enhancing) and participants thought the requirement fair. On the negative side—and in contrast to what the public anticipated—mandatory work programs cost money up-front, for developing worksites, child care, work expenses, monitoring, and enforcement, with little evidence of offsetting savings. That does not mean the work was not useful; in fact, welfare recipients produced services valued at more than the program's cost. But it does mean that mandating work costs much more than simply providing cash benefits. Responding to the need to limit the number of slots and contain child care and other costs, past welfare administrators often required only part-time or short-term work and scheduled assignments around school hours and vacations. They also learned to recycle people into job search and other work-directed services to encourage welfare exits.

Questions about the feasibility and cost of any large-scale effort to implement the work-after-two-years approach are not the only issues. Putting this vision into operation will require addressing other complex questions: Are people paid wages or do they work for benefits? What is the penalty if they do not show up for work? Will there be a time limit on work positions, and, if so, what happens after the limit is reached? How will the time clock be designed and monitored? On each of these issues, there is no obvious right answer, and different state and local administrators will have clear preferences for particular approaches.

How Many People *Can't* Work?

Even the toughest welfare administrators recognize that some welfare recipients face temporary or long-term obstacles to work—substance abuse, learning disabilities, emotional and physical problems, personal crises. For these people, who may not meet strict disability criteria, some fallback system will be needed to protect their children. But distinguishing this group from the able-bodied is hard: some people really cannot work, others could with adequate support. In the past, case-by-case review has been the safety valve, with caseworkers balancing society's twin goals of promoting parents' financial responsibility and protecting children. Should benefits be cut if a mother stays home with a sick child, or if she claims her car broke down or child care fell through, or if a bad back makes her temporarily unemployable? Caseworker discretion has clearly provided loopholes for some but prevented homelessness and hardship for others.

The Success of Job Training

Several California counties have experienced mildly encouraging results operating a new welfare program called GAIN, for Greater Avenues for Independence, and in Riverside the results have been startling.

For two years, the Manpower Development Research Corp. has studied 33,000 people who entered the program between 1988 and 1990. The dramatic findings: Earnings of Riverside participants rose a staggering 55 percent more than earnings of Riverside nonparticipants, earnings rose substantially more than they did in counties that were operating with a different GAIN program, and the cost of welfare decreased an unheard-of 14 percent.

Richard Berman, *Insight on the News*, September 20, 1993.

If, under time-limited welfare, participation demands are tougher, the clamor for exceptions will grow. Having no experience with fully funded work requirements, we know neither how to do this right nor what happens when it is done wrong. States will have to learn the hard way—by doing it—how to balance tougher mandates against protecting needy children. Again, this calls for flexibility and experimentation.

Attitudes toward welfare reform reflect varied views about social justice, equity, the causes of poverty, the role of women, the need to protect children, the goals of reform, and the responsibility of government. These themes play out differently across our diverse nation, with the often-noted result that we do not have one, but fifty, welfare programs. In the 1970s Washington directed welfare-to-work mandates, with little gubernatorial control and anemic implementation. In 1981 Congress gave the states flexibility to redesign these programs, and many governors made welfare reform a state priority, mobilizing resources and shaping programs to meet local objectives. Some states imposed tough work mandates (primarily on men), some provided opportunities for women to get out of poverty, some expanded child care services, some argued that any job was a good job, and others maintained that improved skills were essential for families to leave welfare permanently.

State and local programs tended to deliver on their own objectives—a lesson worth remembering in this new round of reform. In an area as politically charged as welfare reform, staff will vigorously implement programs that meet locally supported goals.

The additional costs and offsetting savings from a system of universal time-limited JOBS mandates followed by a work requirement are not known. Past studies of small-scale programs may understate accomplishments and costs. Furthermore, the enthusiastic public has not had to weigh its interest in making welfare mothers work against its eagerness to pay the bill. In the short term, it is clear that obtaining funds for reform will be a major constraint on implementing this vision, and that there will be a tension between paying for JOBS (upstream) or work positions (downstream).

How Does It All Add Up?

How well program administrators can meet these challenges is not clear. Nor are the likely effects and costs of different solutions. As we enter a new round of reform debates, we are armed with more questions than answers, more ambition than resources.

Current proposals would expand welfare-to-work mandates at a time when the last ones, embodied in the Family Support Act of 1988, are far from fully funded or implemented. For twenty years Congress has favored requiring people to participate in activities leading to a job, but without ever putting up the money to learn whether universal implementation was feasible, let alone what it would accomplish. Repeatedly, the talk has been tough, but the public, looking around five years later, has seen a system largely unchanged.

The record to date suggests a strategy for achieving the re-

170

forms discussed in Congress and by the administration. First, find the funds and provide the technical assistance and know-how to make JOBS' opportunities and mandates real, work-focused, and inevitable for all adult welfare recipients (possibly except those with very young children). This first step would build on and strengthen a program of known effectiveness, put in place a precondition for time limits, and go a long way toward transforming welfare. In the process, experiment with approaches for increasing JOBS' success, particularly in moving very disadvantaged recipients into jobs, a critical step in reducing the number of people reaching the two-year cliff. At the same time, require states to implement JOBS' neglected school attendance mandate for all teen mothers.

Second, reinforce efforts to make work pay and strengthen child support enforcement, experimenting with different techniques to increase the earnings and payments of noncustodial parents. Third, in selected locations around the country, fully fund programs requiring work after a time limit has been reached. Explain to the public that the money is not there to try this everywhere, that time limits are attractive but may prove very costly or put children at risk, and that, given the unknown cost and feasibility, it is prudent to phase in the program before risking the funds and unintended consequences of full-scale national implementation. Invite the nation's governors to develop new ways to operationalize time limits, specifically testing the major alternatives in a variety of environments. Fund the most promising ten to fifteen states at a level sufficient, in at least part of the state, to assure a fair test of this approach: to deliver the child care, develop the work slots, and monitor participation. Provide flexibility for the other states to institute work requirements within JOBS, but under much tighter budget constraints.

If these steps are followed, in five years we will know the answers to the key questions about requiring work after two years on welfare. Is it feasible? Can the jobs be created? How many people can and cannot work? What will it cost? What are the benefits and unintended consequences? What approaches work best? We should also have identified effective strategies to succeed with long-term recipients. And the preconditions—a strong JOBS program and measures to make work pay—will be in place nationwide for expanded implementation, if warranted.

A staged phase-in may disappoint some, but the alternative is welfare reform as usual: an underfunded nationwide program, limited real change, unanswered questions about the potential for success, and a further disillusioned public.

"If the economy isn't creating jobs, . . . training 'only serves to reshuffle the unemployment queue.'"

Job Training Programs Are Ineffective

Spencer Rich

Many welfare reform plans propose job training programs to move welfare recipients into the workforce. In the following viewpoint, Spencer Rich argues that training programs are ineffective unless there are real jobs for those on welfare to obtain. He maintains that most training programs have produced only marginal increases in income for participants, leaving them still miserably poor. Rich is a reporter with the *Washington Post*.

As you read, consider the following questions:

1. In the San Diego welfare experiment cited by Rich, what was the average income for participants compared to nonparticipants?
2. According to the author, what are some reasons that job training will not work for the severely disadvantaged?

President Clinton's plan to "end welfare as we know it" appears to rely heavily on a familiar remedy: two years of education and training for adult recipients after which they would presumably be able to find jobs at decent wages in the private or public sectors.

Certainly the president can find anecdotal support for his proposal in the glowing tales, often reported in the press, of how job training helps welfare mothers and underclass youth transform their lives. Here's one from 1988: Maria Gonzalez, a thirty-three-year-old welfare mother, has found a file clerk job in a Bridgeport, Connecticut, hospital at $14,000 a year plus health insurance, after being trained in a state program. Her earnings will rise with experience.

Here's one from 1991: Two years after participating in a program that included education, training, organized job searches and unpaid work experience, welfare parents in San Diego earned 29 percent more than a control group of similar parents who did not participate.

Stories like these have fueled a popular notion that worker education and training programs are the magic key not only to ending welfare and poverty but also to curing unemployment, unlocking the riches of the economy and guaranteeing good jobs for youth who are not bound for college.

Although Clinton has never specifically promised that job training would bring all these goodies, his campaign rhetoric comes close to doing so: "We ought to tell everybody who gets out of high school who doesn't go to college," he said October 26, 1992, "that if you don't go to college, we'll give you at least two years of further education and training in an apprenticeship program, so you can have a good job, not a dead-end job. You deserve it!"

Job Training Cannot Work Miracles

Whoa! Wait a minute. Remedial education and technical and job training have definitely shown some beneficial results for certain groups of the population. Clinton's proposals could well be a step toward improving the quality of the U.S. workforce and therefore its international competitiveness. But don't expect miracles. For one thing, "training does not create jobs—good ones or bad ones," says Sar Levitan, director of the Center for Social Policy Studies at George Washington University, reflecting a view widely held by training experts and economists. If the economy isn't creating jobs, as a government study put it a few years ago, training "only serves to reshuffle the unemployment queue."

Moreover, virtually every study of government training programs for workers shows that the benefits have been quite modest, particularly in the programs for severely disadvantaged workers where the government puts most of its bucks.

The federal government, according to a report in July 1992 by the General Accounting Office, has "125 federal programs that provide various forms of employment and training assistance to adults and out-of-school youth, with fiscal year 1991 appropriations of $16.3 billion." But government statistics leave little doubt that in the most costly existing programs, which focus on the severely disadvantaged (welfare families, school dropouts, semi-literate unskilled adults and youth), the payoffs are in pennies.

Training Programs Have Limited Success

Don't count on job training. For thirty years, the central canon of welfare reform has been raising skills to raise earnings. But even the most richly funded job-training programs have had only modest success in helping mothers work their way off welfare; none has had any proven success with unwed teen mothers, the core of long-term recipients.

Douglas J. Besharov, *Washington Post National Weekly Edition*, July 31–August 6, 1995.

Two of the best-known programs for the severely disadvantaged—the welfare training programs run by the states and Title II of the Job Training Partnership Act (JTPA)—have been studied extensively. Some of the results are gratifying but far from electrifying. Others are depressing.

Mixed Results for Training Programs

One of the best outcomes ever found in a welfare program was in the San Diego experiment, conducted from 1985 to 1987. The Manpower Demonstration Research Corp. (MDRC), which evaluated this and other welfare-related training programs, found that in the year after completing the program, participants had average earnings 29 percent higher than the control group. The program was found to be cost effective in that savings in reduced welfare payments and the like were almost three times greater than the costs of providing the services.

Well worth doing, but the trainees were still miserably poor despite the gain. Their average income for the second year was $2,903, compared to $2,246 for the control group of nonparticipants. Some, of course, made more, but others less. Moreover, only 49 percent of participants worked at any time during the second year, compared to 40 percent of the control group.

One experiment in six California counties with different combinations of training, education, job-search and other services

174

for single parents on welfare had pretty good results by historical standards, especially in Riverside County. Participants' total
earnings in the first year averaged slightly less than those of nonparticipants in two counties, 15 percent to 18 percent greater in
three counties and a whopping 65 percent greater in Riverside
County.

The Riverside result is so far out of line with results achieved
elsewhere that MDRC cannot fully explain it, and it is possible
the result could not be duplicated. The director of the program,
at a seminar at the American Enterprise Institute, may have in-
advertently offered the best explanation. The first thing he did
each year, he declared, was go to potential employers and lock
up all the available job slots for his "graduates." What this sug-
gested to some listeners was that much of the director's startling
success came from simply grabbing the jobs first—leaving others who might have gotten them unemployed.

But in every one of the six counties, even in Riverside, the total average earnings of the participants, as well as their employment rates, were still appallingly low. In Riverside, the average
participant earned $2,468 in the first year of the program, and
only 33 percent were employed at any time in the first quarter
of the second year.

Training Cannot Replace Welfare

Judith Gueron, MDRC president, says the results show that although many of the welfare training programs "pay for themselves [and] make a difference . . . alone, they will not solve the
problem" of poverty and dependency for many in the welfare
population—and there are about 4 million parents with more
than 8 million children on welfare. Such families will still need
welfare, medical, housing and food aid in many cases.

Another closely evaluated program is the Labor Department's
Job Training Partnership Act Title II program, targeted at low-
income adults and out-of-school youth, on which the government spends about $1.8 billion a year.

"The results are disturbing," says Linda G. Morra, director of
education and employment issues at the General Accounting Office. Assistant director Sigurd Nilsen says, "For youth, the results
are negative. For adults they are positive but marginally so."

The figures, tracing what happened in JTPA from 1987 to 1989,
showed that, compared to a control group of nonparticipants,
adult female enrollees earned about 12 percent more over the
initial eighteen months of the program and adult male enrollees
6.8 percent more. But among out-of-school female youths, earnings were actually slightly less than those of comparable nonparticipants, and among male youths significantly less—11.6 percent less. Anthony Carnevale, chief economist for the American

Society for Training and Development, says one reason the welfare and JTPA results are not better is that in dealing with the severely disadvantaged, "You can't make up for the deficits of a lifetime in a few months of training."

Some enrollees have never worked and are unfamiliar with the idea of arriving at work at a specific time, staying on the job until a specific time and showing up every day. Many can barely read or do simple math and haven't the faintest idea how to look for a job or present themselves to an employer. They have to learn all these things plus job skills.

Under JTPA, the typical enrollee spends up to twenty weeks in a program at a cost of about $2,000, and that may be far too little to prepare them properly. Many state welfare training programs are even more restricted. "You get better results from one to two years of training, using a community college, for example," says one program evaluator, but that costs $6,000 to $7,000 per person, a daunting figure. The Job Corps produces good results with the most severely disadvantaged, but its training is much more intense and also much more costly (about $15,000 per enrollee). Other types of government training programs have shown mixed results. High school vocational education, to which the U.S. government contributes $1.1 billion a year and local governments billions more, produces some immediate advantages for boys who study construction-trade skills and girls who study clerical skills, but the impact fades after six or seven years.

One Promising Area for Training

One area where the impact of training does seem to be good is upgrading the skills of mainstream workers who already have jobs or very good possibilities of finding them, says Samuel Halperin, director of the American Youth Policy Forum, a group concerned with "the forgotten half" of American youth—those who do not go to college.

Studies by the Rand Corp., John H. Bishop of Cornell University and others concluded that training within a company, particularly on-the-job training, has substantial impacts on productivity. Halperin, Nilsen and others say places such as Schneider International, a big trucking firm, Motorola, Saturn and Federal Express have produced excellent results for both the companies and their workers.

That may be why, the welfare initiative aside, Clinton and his secretary of labor, Robert Reich, are focusing heavily not on the severely disadvantaged but on mainstream high school youth who are not going on to a four-year college. The idea is to channel such youths more systematically into community colleges and technical programs to upgrade their basic skills and learn other skills needed in growing areas. The theory behind this ap-

176

proach is enunciated in a book, *America's Choice: High Skills or Low Wages*, put out by a group that included former secretaries of labor Bill Brock and Ray Marshall, Hillary Rodham Clinton ("she was very involved," according to one official), Clinton senior adviser Ira C. Magaziner, Council of Economic Advisers chairman Laura Tyson and others.

Basically it goes like this: America once outproduced the world by breaking "complex jobs into a myriad of simple rote tasks, which the worker then repeats with machine-like efficiency." In that model, only the bosses needed brains, initiative or education. But the world has changed. "What the world is prepared to pay high prices and high wages for now is quality, variety" and quick responsiveness to changing consumer tastes. This change requires that workers and their supervisors cooperate and exchange ideas and that workers be given front-line responsibility "to use judgment and make decisions" and be trained in the use of the most complex machinery and devices.

"Where workers are involved in participating, where they have a voice, you find companies that are much more productive and more profitable," said Reich in January 1993. American firms already spend about $30 billion to train their employees, but Reich points out that $20 billion of this sum is for university graduates.

Apprenticeship Programs in Other Countries

By contrast, in virtually all of the most productive countries, well-organized programs give non-college workers basic reading, math and science tools and technical training beyond high school. About two-thirds of all German youths participate in apprenticeship programs, says Nilsen. In the United States, apprenticeship programs cover less than 2 percent of the non-college labor force, says Carnevale.

It's clear that U.S. firms could benefit from more, or at least better, training efforts for both workers and management. According to several studies, Carnevale says, only 5 percent to 13 percent of U.S. business establishments have adopted the new "high-performance work" orientation. As more companies do—assuming tax and other policies provide the right environment for job expansion—they will need workers with more skills, and that is where worker training comes in. It's an agonizingly slow process to start.

But as the America Youth Policy Forum's Halperin says, "Is there any reason to think American teenagers and young adults not going on to four years of college are dumber and less trainable than their counterparts in Sweden, Denmark, Switzerland or Germany? Obviously not."

"Turn federal programs over to the states where they can be administered more efficiently, at less cost and with more concern for the people involved."

Welfare Should Be Turned Over to the States

John Engler

The governors of many states have recommended ending federal welfare programs and giving the money that is saved to the states to fund their individually designed programs. In the following viewpoint, John Engler, the Republican governor of Michigan, argues that state-run welfare programs would be an improvement over the current system. He contends that while federal programs have failed, state-run experiments have succeeded in reducing welfare rolls and in putting welfare recipients to work. It would be more efficient, Engler maintains, to use federal funds to support these successful state programs than to continue wasting money on the ineffectual federal welfare system.

As you read, consider the following questions:

1. According to Engler, how many Michigan welfare recipients are working compared with the national average?
2. By what percentage have welfare caseloads been reduced in Wisconsin compared with the national average, in the author's words?
3. What is the reason for consolidating federal programs, in the author's opinion?

John Engler, "Welfare Reform: A Question of Hope," *Washington Times*, March 23, 1995. Reprinted with permission.

Republicans in the House of Representatives have introduced a landmark piece of legislation that will completely change the welfare system. We have an unprecedented opportunity to save the lives of millions of children who would otherwise be trapped in a system that condemns them to a life of poverty. But as a governor who has worked to change welfare in my state, I can tell you it won't be easy.

The attacks we have heard from those who would defend the failed status quo have an all-too-familiar ring to them. I, too, was labeled "mean-spirited" and "callous" when I sought to reduce welfare rolls in Michigan. Headlines screamed: "Engler's victory would mean tough times for the needy," and "State abandons the poor." One prominent Democrat official in our state went so far as to suggest that our reforms would incite inner-city riots. My approval ratings sank to a dismal 19 percent.

Change is never easy. But since 1993, as the reforms we proposed have begun to take effect, we have seen positive results. The dire predictions of doom and gloom have proven false, and we are restoring genuine hope to people's lives. We are helping them achieve independence and rediscover the dignity of work. As one welfare recipient who went to work as a result of our reforms told me, "It did not take me long to realize that work is liberation." Today, one out of four welfare recipients in Michigan is working, compared with fewer than one in ten nationwide. As a result, nearly 55,000 cases have been closed due to income from employment, and welfare caseloads have fallen to their lowest level since 1988. In addition, we have saved Michigan taxpayers more than $100 million.

Successful Reform Efforts at the State Level

What we have done in Michigan is but one example of successful welfare-reform efforts taking place in states across the country. Wisconsin Governor Tommy Thompson, who has pioneered a number of innovative reforms, has seen welfare caseloads in his state shrink by 25 percent, compared to a 35 percent increase nationwide. Mr. Thompson is so convinced he can move every welfare recipient into a job that he announced the welfare division of the Wisconsin Social Services Department will be moved to a new Department of Industry, Labor and Job Development. Mr. Thompson said in his State of the State address in January 1995, "Welfare will no longer exist. It will no longer be part of the vocabulary. Welfare is going to be a jobs program."

In the first few months of 1995, Governors Bill Weld of Massachusetts and George Allen of Virginia have passed sweeping welfare reform legislation in their states, and more is coming in states like Georgia, Illinois, Minnesota, Nebraska, Pennsylvania, and Washington. The question is, as *Wall Street Journal* columnist Gerald Seib has described it, "Will the welfare reform debate now raging in Washington fertilize this era of innovation, or smother it just as it blooms?"

As co-chairman of the National Governors' Association's Welfare Reform Leadership Team, I am fortunate to be among a handful of state leaders who have been working closely with House Speaker Newt Gingrich, Senate Majority Leader Bob Dole and members of Congress in a bipartisan effort to establish a plan to end welfare as we know it.

Block Grants Are the Best Solution

I believe that the Republican approach of sending the main control of welfare back to the states by way of block grants is the only—and best—way for this country to go. Many people don't understand what block grants are about. They hear opponents characterize the Republican plan as "abolishing" or "eliminating" programs. But what the block grant approach seeks to do is turn federal programs over to the states where they can be administered more efficiently, at less cost and with more concern for the people involved.

Empower States to Reform Welfare

In California, my administration [as governor] has cut welfare grants 20 percent, saved taxpayers $9 billion, and doubled the number of Californians on Aid to Families with Dependent Children (AFDC) who are now working. But rather than piecemeal efforts to cure our worst ills, the states need authority to recast this failed system and transform it into an entirely new and different one that offers real hope of trading dependency for work, dignity and independence.

Clearly, it's time to remove the shackles of an outdated federal welfare system and give states the freedom we need to determine what is best for our own residents—not the one-size-fits-all edicts from Washington that suit no one.

Pete Wilson, *Washington Times*, December 7, 1995.

There are hundreds of means-tested federal programs. By consolidating some of these, we can cut down on many inane rules and contradictory policies that impede reform. For example, under the current system, if a welfare recipient in Michigan refuses to go to a job training program, and we want to reduce their cash welfare payments as a consequence, that person's food stamps go up automatically. This means there is still no incentive for them to work.

Washington has had sixty years to tackle the welfare problem; now it's time to give the states a chance. We've already proven that we can get results, and certainly we can do better than the current federal system—a dizzying array of failed social experiments that break up families, discourage marriage and don't encourage or reward work. The Republican bill before Congress gives states what Governor Allen calls "the freedom to succeed." It is based on many of the sound principles that we have found successful in changing welfare in our states: requiring work, putting time limits on welfare, discouraging illegitimacy and making deadbeat dads—not the taxpayer—pay to raise their kids.

This legislation gives us an historic opportunity to make lasting and meaningful changes in the welfare system. We must not be deterred by those who have no solutions to offer, only scare tactics. Defenders of the current system will argue that our efforts to change welfare are cruel, but I believe the cruelest punishment of all is to condemn someone to a life on welfare. We cannot allow that to happen to another generation of Americans. We must be bold, we must be creative and we must act now.

"The hidden agenda of the Devolution Revolution [the movement to turn federal social programs over to the states] is a large-scale withdrawal of support for social welfare."

Welfare Should Not Be Turned Over to the States

Daniel Patrick Moynihan

Some reformers have proposed ending federal welfare programs and instead funding state plans with block grants. In the following viewpoint, Daniel Patrick Moynihan, a Democratic senator from New York, defends federal control of welfare, maintaining that under the current system states are already free to experiment with new programs. If states are given control of welfare, Moynihan contends, many will be forced to cut benefits for the poor and for children in order to reduce costs.

As you read, consider the following questions:

1. According to Herman B. Leonard and Monica E. Friar, quoted by the author, what will be profoundly changed by the block grant plan?
2. How many children are on welfare in New York City, according to Moynihan?
3. What is the federal government committed to do under welfare, in Moynihan's view?

A considerable debate has commenced in the Senate, but it is not, as commonly portrayed, about welfare. The subject, rather, is the devolution—"causing to descend"—of social welfare programs from the Federal Government to the states. This takes the form of block grants. It may well prove the next stage in the long, alternating history of federalism.

At issue is the political economy of the New Deal, or at least a goodly portion of it. As a matter of policy, the New Deal brought about a great shift in resources from the North to the South and West. At the same time, New Deal policies brought a great measure of support for the dependent poor, not least in New York State (which, adjusting the cost of living, now has the sixth highest poverty rate in the nation). Devolution might ease the former problem while hugely worsening the latter.

The Devolution Revolution

Professors Herman B. Leonard and Monica E. Friar of the Kennedy School of Government at Harvard comment that the changes wrought by block grants may be small at first but that "these proposals amount to profound structural changes in the funding mechanisms underlying the programs and therefore will likely result in profound changes in the spending trajectory."

On July 27, 1995, in testimony before the Senate Finance Committee, Richard P. Nathan of the Rockefeller Institute of Government in Albany coined the name for the change: the Devolution Revolution of 1995. It would be, he said, far more consequential than the Great Society. He elaborated: "As economist Joseph Schumpeter once said . . . it is in fiscal issues like this that you can hear the thundering hoofbeats of history."

Well, Schumpeter could. It's harder for the rest of us, but surely not that hard. Take welfare. Aid to Families with Dependent Children began with the Social Security Act of 1935 as a widow's pension, pending the time when Survivors Insurance would take over. But a new class of dependent families appeared, young mothers either unmarried, separated or divorced.

In New York City today, more than half a million children are on welfare at any one time, and more than half of all children will be at some time. The racial and ethnic component of this change inhibited open discussion in the 1960s and 70s. But mostly the problem was that at the time the welfare departments didn't recognize that they were dealing with something new.

There is a Law of Retarded Response. Political change often comes abruptly. But there is a lag in grasping social change. By 1988, the welfare bureaucracies had caught up—enough so that in the Senate, by a vote of 96 to 1, A.F.D.C. was redefined as a form of temporary assistance, with a wholly new emphasis on getting a job and becoming self-supporting. The states were encouraged to experiment, innovate, evaluate. In fact, some were already doing so.

Now to something crucial. Welfare is not an entitlement to individuals. It is a commitment by the Federal Government to match state spending on programs that states devise. Individuals must be treated equally, says the Social Security Act, but states can provide whatever benefits they choose. Indeed, they can choose to provide nothing.

Clay Bennett/North America Syndicate. Used with permission.

A Federal waiver process obscures the fact that there is no individual entitlement, but it needn't. Virginia recently asked for a waiver to limit eligibility for A.F.D.C. to two years. Two years and out! On July 1, 1995, President Clinton approved, saying, "It's a good plan, and I'm proud to be supporting it." Wisconsin is planning to end A.F.D.C. altogether by the end of 1997. Entirely doable under present law.

Race to End Welfare

Another little-noticed aspect of the present debate is that conservative critics of the previous welfare system, before the Family Support Act, are demonstrably alarmed at what is being proposed. On March 9, 1995, Lawrence Mead, a professor at Princeton's Woodrow Wilson School, a conservative, told the

Senate Finance Committee, "To improve welfare, I believe, requires changing the Federal role, not abandoning it."

The hidden agenda of the Devolution Revolution is a large-scale withdrawal of support for social welfare, no matter how well conceived. The result would be a race to the bottom, as states, deprived of Federal matching funds, compete with one another to reduce spending by depriving their own dependent population of help.

Such an outcome was projected by the economists Thomas Grannemann and Mark Pauly in 1983 after conducting careful simulations to determine how states would respond to block grants. In New York, they concluded, spending per poor person would drop by half.

The nation is straying into the unknown here. Consider the matter of out-of-wedlock births. A steadily growing percentage of children are born into single-parent homes, and many of these will become dependent on welfare. Some think the answer is simple: repeal Title IV-A (A.F.D.C.) of the Social Security Act and eliminate welfare benefits.

It is an argument that James Q. Wilson, professor of management and public policy at the University of California at Los Angeles, describes as "in large measure based on untested assumptions, ideological posturing and perverse priorities."

"We are told that ending A.F.D.C. will reduce illegitimacy," he said in a speech, "but we don't know that. It is, at best, an informed guess."

The voices being heard on behalf of the children just now have been thought of as conservatives in the past. Liberals would do well to listen to them today.

"Demanding personal responsibility in return for a welfare check only makes sense."

Welfare Reform Should Promote Personal Responsibility

Tommy G. Thompson

Conservative reformers have proposed time limits on receiving aid as a way to discourage long-term welfare dependency. In the following viewpoint, Tommy G. Thompson, the Republican governor of Wisconsin, argues that strict time limits on benefits are a necessary part of the plan to encourage welfare recipients to find work and to support themselves and their families. If government provides educational and job-training programs along with benefits, Thompson contends, then recipients must exercise the responsibility to become self-supporting.

As you read, consider the following questions:

1. According to Thompson, what is the reason for the complete failure of the current welfare system?
2. What is the reasoning behind the Children First program, in the author's words?
3. What benefits will people receive under the Work Not Welfare program, according to the author? How long does he say they will receive these benefits?

Tommy G. Thompson, "Response and Responsibility: Welfare Reform That Works," *Commonsense*, Spring 1994. Reprinted with permission.

Does personal behavior play a role in the crises facing America today? Myron Magnet in "Emancipating the Underclass," published in the Winter 1994 issue of *Commonsense*, argued that it most certainly does.

On the other hand, those on the left have argued for years that the underlying cause for society's most persistent problems—welfare dependency, crime, drug-abuse, and homelessness—is economics. Unfair economic conditions created these problems, and more fair and equitable economic conditions are the only way to solve them. Behavior never really enters into the equation as a root cause.

Economics and Behavior

I don't believe you can separate the two. Economics and personal behavior must be the top two priorities if your goal is to help people help themselves. That is the goal of welfare reform in Wisconsin and that is why our reforms have a two-pronged approach—providing economic opportunity and requiring personal responsibility at the same time.

You have to expect personal responsibility from the very beginning or you are never going to succeed. The complete failure of the current welfare system can be traced to the fact that the system gives money to people and doesn't ask for a single thing in return. Nothing. Any system that is set up that way is bound to fail. And it has—miserably.

In Wisconsin, we are trying to make welfare more like the real world, and in the real world people have to take responsibility for their actions. If you bring children into this world, it is your responsibility to provide for those children and care for those children. If you are on AFDC (Aid to Families with Dependent Children) and you have additional children, you should not receive additional cash benefits for that. If you want to improve your economic situation, it is your responsibility to get the training and education you will need to do so. We shouldn't expect less of people simply because they are on welfare.

The government's role in all of this is to be a partner. *Response and responsibility.* If we are going to give you a check, then we are going to expect certain things in return. If we provide job training and the transportation to get there, it is your responsibility to attend. If we provide day care, it is your responsibility to sign up for a job, get up every morning, and go to work. If you are supporting your children on welfare, you have to make sure those children attend school regularly.

This kind of approach is simple commonsense. And commonsense is at the very root of all the welfare reforms we are trying in Wisconsin.

Our first step in welfare reform was to establish a comprehensive job-training program to give people on welfare the skills they need to get a job and become productive members of society. Our Workfare program served as a model for the national JOBS (Job Opportunities and Basic Skills Training) program.

Our second key reform was Learnfare. Learnfare is simple; if you are a high school student and you or your family receive AFDC benefits, you will go to school. If you don't, your welfare benefits will be cut. Forty-eight percent of Wisconsin's current welfare recipients do not have a high school degree. It only makes sense to make sure today's generation receives the education it needs to escape the welfare trap. We recently expanded Learnfare to include students between the ages of six and twelve, so children learn from a young age that going to school is a requirement, not an option.

Encouraging Responsibility

In a tough bill that my task force [Shaw is a congressional representative from Florida] on welfare has introduced, we time-limit Aid to Families with Dependent Children (AFDC), require training and/or work for able-bodied recipients, discourage illegitimacy, and mandate paternity establishment.

We encourage parental responsibility and ask states to impose strict requirements and penalties for welfare recipients who fail to meet standards. And we find a way to pay for it without increased taxes.

E. Clay Shaw Jr., *American Legion*, July 1994.

In Wisconsin, we believe that *both* parents are responsible for the children they bring into this world, and we are a national leader in collecting child support. One of the reasons is an innovative program called Children First. Like our other welfare reforms, Children First is very simple: if you are a non-custodial parent (this is most often the father), you are responsible for the financial support of your children. If you are not paying your way, we give you a choice—either find a job or go to jail. If you can't find a job, we will find one for you in the community work experience program. You can work as a crossing guard, for example, or sweep up at the courthouse. It's amazing how quickly people find jobs when they are faced with this choice. In the first two counties where Children First began, child support collections have increased by 132 percent. We now plan to expand the program to seven more counties.

Wisconsin is also working to eliminate the current welfare

system's disincentives to work and forming two-parent families. We were one of the first states to receive a waiver from the federal 100-hour rule, which allows AFDC recipients to work more without losing AFDC benefits. Our Parental and Family Responsibility Initiative removes marriage penalties for young parents who want to raise their child in a two-parent household. It also requires fathers to assume greater responsibility for their children, and limits AFDC grant increases for additional children.

Time Limits for Welfare

Our most recent pilot program is called Work Not Welfare, and it started in two counties in January 1995. Under this program, people who sign up for welfare will receive checks for two years, along with extensive education and job training, free child and health care. During the two-year period, they will have to work or train in exchange for their welfare check. After two years, the welfare checks—the cash benefits—will end. No more indefinite entitlement, no more long-term dependency. If you want cash, you're going to have to work for it.

Work Not Welfare is on the cutting edge of a whole new way of looking at how to really help the disadvantaged in our society. And Wisconsin isn't going to stop there. In December 1993, I signed legislation that will effectively end welfare in the state of Wisconsin. As of January 1, 1999, the state's basic welfare program—Aid to Families with Dependent Children—will cease to exist. Between then and now, we will develop a replacement system that is pro-work, pro-family, and pro-child. And it will not be an indefinite entitlement.

Providing economic opportunity for welfare recipients is only one part of helping them become self-sufficient members of society. As Myron Magnet wrote in his article, "economic opportunity is meaningful only if individuals are culturally equipped to seize it." Demanding personal responsibility in return for a welfare check only makes sense. It makes welfare more like the real world, and—if we are successful—the real world is where these welfare recipients are going to be working and raising their families in the future.

"Curtailing benefits without first reducing the need for assistance hurts children, . . . perpetuates the cycle of poverty, and may force families to live on the streets."

Welfare Reform Should Serve the Needs of the Poor

Lynn Woolsey

Concerned with breaking long-term dependence on welfare aid, some reformers have proposed two-year limits on benefits. In the following two-part viewpoint, Lynn Woolsey, a Democratic congresswoman from Petaluma, California, maintains that a time limit on benefits would be devastating to poor welfare recipients and their children. Describing her own experience as a welfare mother, she contends that the aid she received was necessary for her to overcome her temporary state of poverty.

As you read, consider the following questions:

1. In Woolsey's opinion, why was she more fortunate than most welfare clients?
2. What are the elements of a fair and just welfare system, according to the author?

Lynn Woolsey, "Living on Welfare—a Personal View," *Social Justice*, vol. 21, no. 1, Spring 1994, p. 87-88. Reprinted by permission. Lynn Woolsey, "Reinvent Welfare, Humanely," *New York Times*, January 22, 1994. Copyright 1994 by The New York Times Company. Reprinted by permission.

I

When I was running for office, I made my story public about having been a single mother on welfare. I have had movie offers, book offers, and now a made-for-TV offer—all of which I put aside as a member of Congress. Now I think that if I am re-elected, I may pursue this because of the message it conveys about the life of a typical welfare mother. When I was on welfare, I received much more than women do today. Still, I was the mother of three small children, married to a man who was very successful but who was mentally ill and wouldn't get help. So I am a survivor. My kids and I were without resources and we had to change our lives. I would have liked to work, but since I had children, I intended to be a mother. After all, I grew up in the 1950s when housekeeping was the rule of thumb. I was to be a mother and that was the way it was.

Welfare Is Necessary

I went to work and soon found that earning $580 a month was not going to support my three small children and myself. Thus, I sold my house before it was repossessed, returned my brand new car and got a VW beetle, and moved into a two-bedroom cottage. A very good friend of mine moved me into that cottage. I realized that I still could not cover the costs of necessities for my children and me; we needed health care and child care was a problem the first year. So I went on Aid to Families with Dependent Children. I was never embarrassed by it; I simply had to have it. My friends would ask me how I could be on welfare and my answer was, "Well, I need it and I'm not embarrassed." I realize how much more fortunate I am than most welfare clients. I can speak English, I'm educated—I have two years of college—and I was certain that I deserved it. It never entered my mind that I wasn't going to get everything that was available to us.

How, then, did I get off welfare? First I was employed, underpaid by what eventually became a Fortune 500 company. I began as the office manager. Years later, when I left, we had 700 employees and I was the Human Resources Director. I also married one of my co-workers, who was a single parent, and we put a life together for our four children. That was the combination it took for me to be successful. There was one more element, and it was probably as important as the first two. The first year I went to work I had thirteen child care situations. My friend Carol would back me up when one of my child care workers wouldn't show up. That was the worst year for me and for my children. My child care situation only stabilized when I remarried, was living in Petaluma, California, and brought my mother from Seattle to live in Petaluma. My mother came to our house every day when the children came home from school. That was the year I was promoted to management. There was no way, until then, that I could concentrate all of my brain on making a living. That was twenty-five years ago, and I have never forgotten that I got off welfare. I needed a great deal of help, however, and so do many other people. I think that is what government is for. I also believe that welfare must be reformed to make the system just, and that topic commands our attention now.

II

It's time to end welfare as I knew it.

Twenty-five years ago I was a single, working mother, unable to provide for my three children, ages one, three and five. I know what it is like to lie awake at night and worry about not having any health insurance. I know how hard it is to find good child care—I had thirteen different babysitters in one year. I know what it is like to choose between paying the rent and buying new shoes.

Like so many American families, we turned to Aid to Families with Dependent Children.

How Women Leave Welfare

Percentage of welfare departures in 1993.

Unidentified 24%

Work gave enough income 46%

Disability 1%

Moved between states 2%

No longer eligible child in household 3%

Moved in with family or friends 5%

Non-work-related income increase 7%

Marriage, remarriage or reconciliation 11%

New York Times, June 19, 1994.

As the only former welfare mother ever to serve in Congress, I know firsthand the merits and faults of our welfare system. And I know we must create a fair and just system that would provide families with the tools they need to get off welfare and become self-sufficient.

Sadly, the ideas that seem to be gaining ground these days are misguided or worse. Proposals like that of the social scientist Charles Murray—which would abolish everything from food stamps to subsidized housing—would starve families only to feed alarmist myths about welfare. Such brutal proposals would have devastated my family. The denial of essential services would rip the safety net from under families in temporary need and burn the ladder to self-sufficiency for those trapped in long-term poverty.

Time limits on welfare benefits, the centerpiece of both Democratic and Republican proposals, would be just as damaging to families. While the purpose—to move individuals off welfare and into the work force—is laudable, a rigid approach is unworkable. The proposal by Governor William F. Weld of Massachusetts, to cut off benefits after sixty days for all able-bodied recipients who did not accept full-time community service jobs at less than the minimum wage, is a case in point: curtailing benefits without first reducing the need for assistance hurts children, who account for 70 percent of welfare recipients; it perpetuates the cycle of poverty, and may force families to live on the streets.

A More Just Proposal

My own vision of a just and fair welfare system is based on experience, not theory. Here is what it would do:

- Establish Federal job-training programs that would insure self-sufficiency.
- Overhaul our child-support system by stiffening enforcement and guaranteeing that all families receive a minimum level of payment.
- Abolish financial penalties against two-parent families.
- Encourage welfare recipients to work by allowing them to keep more of their earnings and benefits.
- Provide a full range of support services like child care, health care and counseling, as well as qualified case management.
- Build partnerships of labor, business and government to create jobs that pay a living wage.

Make no mistake: welfare reform will cost money in the short term. But it will reap long-term results. The Clinton Administration wants a welfare plan that doesn't increase the deficit. I want a plan that works. We must craft a plan that both respects the budget and achieves our common goal for financial independence for all American families.

This debate is about what we value as a nation. I turned to welfare so I could take care of my children. Now we must fix the welfare system to make sure all of our children are given the care they need.

Periodical Bibliography

The following articles have been selected to supplement the diverse views presented in this chapter. Addresses are provided for periodicals not indexed in the *Readers' Guide to Periodical Literature*, the *Alternative Press Index*, or the *Social Sciences Index*.

Alan Ehrenhalt	"Out in the States, It's Not the 1930s Anymore," *Governing*, December 1995.
John Engler	"No Devil in Devolution," *National Review*, August 28, 1995.
David Frum	"Building Blocks," *American Spectator*, May 1995.
Penelope Lemov	"Putting Welfare on the Clock," *Governing*, November 1993.
Daniel Patrick Moynihan	"Congress Builds a Coffin," *New York Review of Books*, January 11, 1996.
National Review	"Worse Than No Bill," October 9, 1995.
Paul Offner	"Flippers," *New Republic*, February 12, 1996.
Robert Rector	"Stringing Along," *National Review*, April 17, 1995.
Paul Craig Roberts	"Welfare: Maybe the States Can Figure Out What Works," *Business Week*, December 4, 1995.
Robert J. Samuelson	"The Politics of Ignorance," *Newsweek*, December 18, 1995.
Robert J. Samuelson	"Welfare Can't Be Reformed," *Newsweek*, March 27, 1995.
Robert A. Sirico	"Ethics and the Budget Debate," *Forbes*, February 26, 1996.
Daniel T. Wackerman	"Mind's Eye," *America*, January 13–20, 1996.
Jacob Weisberg	"How Low Can You Go?" *New York*, January 15, 1996.

For Further Discussion

Chapter 1

1. Clarissa Pinkola Estés describes how welfare once helped her to support herself and her young child. In his viewpoint, Bill Clinton contends that the welfare system must be reformed to help recipients get off welfare. How would Clinton respond to Estés's contention that welfare reform would deny essential services to the poor?

2. Valerie Polakow writes that many single mothers lack access to affordable child care. George Liebmann argues that maternity homes can care for both poor mothers and their children. How would the women interviewed by Polakow react to the prospect of living in a maternity home? Use the women's testimony to support your answer.

3. Marvin Olasky maintains that poor Americans need compassionate care and that private charities can provide it more effectively than the government. Catholic Charities USA president Fred Kammer argues that many private charities will be unable to care for the poor without government funding. Whose argument is more effective? Why?

Chapter 2

1. Chris Tilly and Randy Albelda argue that low hourly wages and high unemployment rates force poor women to rely on welfare. Michael Tanner, Stephen Moore, and David Hartman contend that many welfare recipients enjoy generous benefits that total more than the salary from a well-paying, full-time job. Which authors make the more convincing argument? Why?

2. In their viewpoints, Pat Rowe, Douglas J. Besharov, and Karen N. Gardiner describe voluntary and mandatory programs aimed at making poor teenage mothers self-sufficient. List the positive and negative aspects of voluntary and mandatory approaches to keeping individuals in school, teaching personal responsibility, and improving employment skills. Explain your reasoning.

Chapter 3

1. Rachel Wildavsky and Daniel R. Levine profile three welfare mothers. According to the authors, what are the different types of assistance that each woman receives? How much money does each receive? In Rita Henley Jensen's account,

what type of assistance and how much money does the average welfare mother receive? How do the authors' views affect their conclusions?

2. Paul Offner contends that the costs of providing welfare to children could be reduced if the federal government collected child support from nonpaying "deadbeat dads." In Jenifer Rachel's opinion, why would children not benefit from such a plan? Who would benefit, according to Rachel? With which author do you agree more? Why?

3. Robert Rector and William F. Lauber argue that elderly immigrants should not receive welfare benefits. According to the authors, what is the cost of providing benefits to these immigrants? In Julian L. Simon's estimate, what is the cost of providing benefits to immigrants? In your opinion, should elderly immigrants be eligible for welfare benefits? Defend your answer using examples from the viewpoints.

Chapter 4

1. Mimi Abramovitz argues that conservative welfare reform measures are unfair because they attempt to change or control the behavior of women. In Douglas J. Besharov's opinion, what is the key to reforming the welfare system? How do work and training programs achieve this goal, according to Besharov? What arguments does Abramovitz present in opposition to work and training programs? With which author's arguments do you agree more? Defend your answer using examples from the viewpoints.

2. John Engler argues that state-run welfare programs have succeeded, whereas federal programs have failed. What evidence does he present to support this contention? What evidence does Daniel Patrick Moynihan present to demonstrate the successfulness of federal welfare programs? Which author's use of evidence do you find more effective? Why?

3. Tommy G. Thompson argues that if the government provides welfare benefits to people, it has the right to demand personal responsibility from them. What programs does he outline as a way to promote personal responsibility? In Lynn Woolsey's view, what elements would constitute a fair and just welfare system? What programs does she propose? Which programs would you support? Why?

Organizations to Contact

The editors have compiled the following list of organizations concerned with the issues debated in this book. The descriptions are derived from materials provided by the organizations. All have publications or information available for interested readers. The list was compiled on the date of publication of the present volume; names, addresses, phone and fax numbers, and e-mail addresses may change. Be aware that many organizations take several weeks or longer to respond to inquiries, so allow as much time as possible.

Bread for the World
National Office
1100 Wayne Ave., Suite 1000
Silver Spring, MD 20910
(301) 608-2400
fax: (301) 608-2401

Bread for the World is a nonpartisan Christian citizens movement that works to end world hunger. It also concentrates on issues related to hunger, such as domestic poverty, agriculture, and unemployment. Its members lobby congressional representatives and other government leaders regarding U.S. policies that affect the poor. The organization publishes the newsletter *Bread* eight times a year, the *Background Paper* five times a year, and the paper "Let's Get Real About Welfare."

Cato Institute
1000 Massachusetts Ave. NW
Washington, DC 20001-5403
(202) 842-0200
fax: (202) 842-3490

The Cato Institute is a libertarian public policy research foundation dedicated to promoting traditional American principles of limited government, individual liberty, and peace. The institute advocates abolishing all government welfare programs and returning charity to the private sector. It publishes the triannual *Cato Journal*, the bimonthly newsletter *Cato Policy Report*, and the quarterly magazine *Regulation*.

Economic Policy Institute (EPI)
1600 L St. NW, Suite 1200
Washington, DC 20036
(202) 775-8810
fax: (202) 775-0819

EPI conducts research and provides a forum for the exchange of information on economic policy. It promotes educational programs to encourage discussion of economic policy and economic issues, particularly the economics of poverty, unemployment, inflation, American industry, international competitiveness, and problems of economic adjustment as they affect the community and the individual. EPI publishes the periodic *Briefing Papers*, the triannual *EPI Journal*, and the biennial *State of Working America*.

Employment and Training Institute
University of Wisconsin Center for Continuing Education
161 W. Wisconsin Ave., Suite 6000
Milwaukee, WI 53203
internet: http://www.uwm.edu/Dept/ETI/

The University of Wisconsin-Milwaukee Employment and Training Institute provides applied research, evaluation, policy planning, and technical assistance for local and state governments, community organizations, and national agencies. Its research focuses on interrelationships between labor market changes, employment training programs, education programs, and welfare policies in urban areas. The institute has a variety of reports available on the internet.

Fair Budget Action Campaign
PO Box 31151
Seattle, WA 98103
(206) 727-0369
fax: (206) 727-0358

The campaign works to combat poverty and to help low-income people express their needs and opinions in public forums. It seeks to achieve these goals by educating the public, the media, and policymakers about issues of economic justice. The campaign publishes numerous fact sheets, including "Welfare: Myths and Facts" and "The Gap Continues to Grow."

The Foundation for Economic Education (FEE)
30 S. Broadway
Irvington-on-Hudson, NY 10533
(914) 591-7230
fax: (914) 591-8910
e-mail: freeman@westnet.com

FEE is an educational foundation that promotes the principles of private property, the free market, limited constitutional government, individual responsibility, free enterprise, and the rule of law. It opposes government assistance of any kind. Among its publications are the monthly journal *Freeman: Ideas on Liberty*, the bimonthly newsletter *Notes from FEE*, and numerous books.

The Heritage Foundation
214 Massachusetts Ave. NE
Washington, DC 20002
(202) 546-4400
fax: (202) 546-0904
web site: http://www.townhall.com

The foundation is a conservative public policy research institute dedicated to the principles of free, competitive enterprise, limited government, individual liberty, and a strong national defense. It advocates serious reform of the welfare system in such areas as controlling rising welfare costs and reducing illegitimacy. Among the foundation's numerous publications are the quarterly journal *Policy Review*, the book *America's Failed $5.4 Trillion War on Poverty*, and the papers "Addressing Illegitimacy: The Root of Real Welfare Reform" and "Why Congress Must Reform Welfare."

HUD USER
U.S. Department of Housing and Urban Development
PO Box 6091
Rockville, MD 20849
(301) 251-5154
(800) 245-2691
fax: (301) 251-5747
e-mail: huduser@aspensys.com
web site: http://www.aspensys.com:84/huduser.html

HUD USER is a research information service and clearinghouse for people working toward improving housing and strengthening community development. It collects, develops, and distributes housing-related information. The organization publishes the three-volume *Operation Bootstrap*, the report "Regionalism: The New Geography of Opportunity," and numerous other welfare-related publications.

NOW Legal Defense and Education Fund
99 Hudson St.
New York, NY 10013-2815
(212) 925-6635
fax: (212) 226-1066

The fund is the educational and litigating arm of the National Organization for Women. As such, it provides legal assistance to women and employs legal action, education, and community-based projects to combat discrimination based on sex. The fund publishes the quarterly newsletter *In Brief* and the reports "A Leadership Summit: The Link Between Violence and Poverty in the Lives of Women and Their Children" and "Welfare and Out-of-Wedlock Births: A Research Summary."

Office for Church in Society
United Church of Christ
110 Maryland Ave. NE, Suite 207
Washington, DC 20002
(202) 543-1517
fax: (202) 543-5994

An agency of the United Church of Christ, the office directs the theological and ethical resources of the church toward social action programs and information. It believes that government welfare programs should be designed to help children in poverty, whatever the circumstances of their parents. It also promotes the involvement of religious institutions in providing charity and emergency relief services to the poor. The office publishes the newsletter *Courage in the Struggle for Justice and Peace* ten times a year.

Poverty and Race Research Action Council (PRRAC)
1711 Connecticut Ave. NW, Suite 207
Washington, DC 20009
(202) 387-9887
fax: (202) 387-0764

PRRAC was established by a coalition of civil rights, antipoverty, and legal services groups. It works to develop new antiracism and antipoverty strategies and provides funding for research projects that support advocacy work. It publishes the bimonthly *Poverty and Race* and the book *Double Exposure: Poverty and Race in America.*

Progressive Policy Institute (PPI)
518 C St. NE
Washington, DC 20002
(202) 547-0001
fax: (202) 544-5014
internet: ppiinfo@dlcppi.org

PPI develops policy alternatives to the conventional Left-Right political debate. It advocates social policies that move beyond merely maintaining the poor to liberating them from poverty and dependency. It publishes the position paper "GOP Cuts in the EITC: Raising Taxes on the Working Poor," which addresses the issue of the earned income tax credit.

Reason Foundation
3415 S. Sepulveda Blvd., Suite 400
Los Angeles, CA 90034
(310) 391-2245
fax: (310) 391-4395

The foundation works to provide a better understanding of the intellectual basis of a free society and to develop new ideas in public policymaking. It researches contemporary social, economic, urban, and political problems. The foundation believes that welfare has become a destructive, multigenerational lifestyle that burdens working Americans with higher taxes. It publishes the newsletter *Privatization Watch* monthly and *Reason* magazine eleven times a year.

Bibliography of Books

Louise Armstrong — *Of "Sluts" and "Bastards": A Feminist Decodes the Welfare Debate.* Monroe, ME: Common Courage Press, 1995.

Mary Jo Bane and David T. Ellwood — *Welfare Realities: From Rhetoric to Reform.* Cambridge, MA: Harvard University Press, 1994.

Jill Duerr Berrick — *Faces of Poverty: Portraits of Women and Children on Welfare.* New York: Oxford University Press, 1995.

Helen Blank and Nicole Poersch — *The Welfare Reform Debate: Implications for Child Care.* Washington, DC: Children's Defense Fund, 1996.

George J. Borjas — *Immigration and Welfare, 1970–1990.* Cambridge, MA: National Bureau of Economic Research, 1994.

Tony Cutler and Barbara Waine — *Managing the Welfare State: The Politics of Public Management.* New York: Oxford University Press, 1994.

Nicholas Deakin — *The Politics of Welfare: Continuities and Change.* New York: Harvester Wheatsheaf, 1994.

Hartley Dean — *Welfare, Law, and Citizenship.* New York: Prentice Hall, 1996.

Daniel Friedlander and Gary Burtless — *Five Years After: The Long-Term Effects of Welfare-to-Work Programs.* New York: Russell Sage Foundation, 1995.

Herbert J. Gans — *The War Against the Poor: The Underclass and Antipoverty Policy.* New York: BasicBooks, 1995.

Neil Gilbert — *Welfare Justice: Rethinking Social Equity.* New Haven, CT: Yale University Press, 1995.

Linda Gordon — *Pitied but Not Entitled: Single Mothers and the History of Welfare.* New York: Free Press, 1994.

Peter Gottschalk and Robert A. Moffitt — *Welfare Dependence: Concepts, Measures, and Trends.* Madison, WI: Institute for Research on Poverty, 1994.

Joel Handler — *The Poverty of Welfare Reform.* New Haven, CT: Yale University Press, 1995.

Lingxin Hao — *Kin Support, Welfare, and Out-of-Wedlock Mothers.* New York: Garland, 1994.

Michael B. Katz	*Improving Poor People: The Welfare State, the "Underclass," and Urban Schools as History.* Princeton, NJ: Princeton University Press, 1995.
Jonathan Kozol	*Amazing Grace: The Lives of Children and the Conscience of a Nation.* New York: Crown, 1995.
Mike Males	*The Scapegoat Generation.* Monroe, ME: Common Courage Press, 1996.
David Marsland, ed.	*Self Reliance: Reforming Welfare in Advanced Societies.* New Brunswick, NJ: Transaction, 1995.
Marjorie Mayo	*Communities and Caring: The Mixed Economy of Welfare.* New York: St. Martin's Press, 1994.
Lawrence M. Mead	*Welfare Reform and Children.* Cambridge, MA: Harvard University Press, 1994.
R. Shep Melnick	*Between the Lines: Interpreting Welfare Rights.* Washington, DC: Brookings Institution, 1994.
William C. Mitchell and Randy T. Simmons	*Beyond Politics: Markets, Welfare, and the Failure of Bureaucracy.* Boulder, CO: Westview Press, 1994.
Donald F. Norris and Lyke Thompson	*The Politics of Welfare Reform.* Newbury Park, CA: Sage, 1995.
Ann Oakley and A. Susan Williams	*The Politics of the Welfare State.* London: UCL Press, 1994.
Jill S. Quadagno	*The Color of Welfare: How Racism Undermined the War on Poverty.* New York: Oxford University Press, 1994.
Mark Robert Rank	*Living on the Edge: The Realities of Welfare in America.* New York: Columbia University Press, 1994.
Nancy Ellen Rose	*Workfare or Fair Work: Women, Welfare, and Government Work Programs.* New Brunswick, NJ: Rutgers University Press, 1995.
Isabel V. Sawhill, ed.	*Welfare Reform: An Analysis of the Issues.* Washington, DC: Urban Institute, 1995.
Virginia E. Schein	*Working from the Margins: Voices of Mothers in Poverty.* Ithaca, NY: ILR Press, 1995.
Sanford Schram	*Words of Welfare: The Poverty of Social Science and the Social Science of Poverty.* Minneapolis: University of Minnesota Press, 1995.
Roberta Spalter-Roth et al.	*Welfare That Works: The Working Lives of AFDC Recipients.* Washington, DC: Institute for Women's Policy Research, 1995.

Index

Aber, J. Lawrence, 93
abortion, 55, 108
Abramovitz, Mimi, 157
Abt Associates, 98, 101
Act for Better Child Care, 33
Administration for Children and
  Families (ACF)
  Office of Family Assistance (OFA),
    90, 95
adoption, 41, 50, 55
African Americans, 86, 116, 119, 155
Aid for Families with Dependent
  Children (AFDC), 20, 45, 67, 81, 143
  cash grants are small, 47, 117–18
    and declining, 26, 70
  and child support collection, 127–28
  cut in Wisconsin, 43–44, 184
  and dependency, 38, 84
  effect of reforms on women/
    children, 159
  federal and state run, 124
  history of, 52, 79, 158, 165, 183
  is one of several welfare benefits, 77
  1988 amendments to, 53
  and paternity procedures, 130, 159,
    160
  recipients of, 97, 107–13
  and shame, 115, 120
  see also single mothers; teen
    mothers; welfare
Alaska, 80, 81, 92
  and wage-equivalent welfare
    benefits, 76, 77, 78, 82
Albelda, Randy, 83
alcohol/drug abuse, 59, 60, 99, 107,
  110–11
  can be reduced by religious
    programs, 63
Allen, George, 179, 181
American Enterprise Institute, 175
American Hebrew, 61
American Legion, 188
American Society for Training and
  Development, 176
America Youth Policy Forum, 176, 177
Anderson, Martin, 41
Archer, Bill, 25
Arenson, Karen W., 67
Arizona, 91, 92
Arkansas, 92

Bane, Mary Jo, 90

Barnes, Peter, 19
Bennett, William, 155
Berman, Richard, 169
Bernstein, Jared, 86
Besharov, Douglas J., 96, 153, 174
Bishop, John H., 176
Bradley, Bill, 50, 54
Britain, 30, 31, 58
Brock, Bill, 177
Brock, Thomas, 156
Brooks-Gunn, Jeane, 93
Brumberg, J.J., 51
Bush, George, 159
  administration, 143

California, 55, 154, 180, 191
  and child support enforcement,
    128–29
  and mandatory work programs, 99,
    154, 166, 169, 174–75
  Pregnancy Freedom of Choice Act,
    54
Carnevale, Anthony, 175, 177
Carter, Jimmy, 167
Catholic Charities, 66, 67, 69
Cato Institute, 147
Census Bureau, 129, 130
Center for Social Policy Studies, 173
Center on Budget and Policy
  Priorities, 86
charitable aid
  cannot replace government
    welfare, 65–71
  should be linked to family
    responsibility, 60
  should replace government welfare,
    41, 51, 56–64
  works in partnership with
    government, 67–69
child care, 25, 84, 87, 95, 161
  costs of, 26, 45, 46
  crisis in, 44
  demands of, on women, 84–86,
    119, 191–92
  is needed to facilitate work/training
    programs, 95, 168
  should be subsidized for more
    families, 31–32, 33
Children's Rights Council (CRC), 130
child support, 27, 86
  enforced payment of, 24, 156,
    161, 188

does not benefit children, 127–28
should be required of noncustodial fathers, 122–25
is mostly paid by noncustodial
fathers, 126–31
reform needed for, 130–31
Child Trends, Inc., 97
Christian Science Monitor, 148
Clark, Rebecca, 137, 138
Clean and Sober Streets, 63
Clinton, Bill, 22, 36, 84, 154
administration, 127, 130, 141, 193
health care plan, 27–28, 30, 32–33
welfare reform plan, 22–26, 123,
124, 155
relies on effectiveness of job
training, 173
and time-limits welfare for
nonworkers, 45, 84, 154, 184
as unfair to women, 158
would convert welfare into
reciprocal obligation, 166–67
and focus on highschoolers, 176
and tax reforms, 118–19
uses welfare issue for political
credit, 121
vetoed Republican Responsibility
Act, 45
Clinton, Hillary Rodham, 177
Coalition of Parent Support, 129
Commission on Drug and Alcohol
Abuse, 63
Commission on Interstate Child
Support, 123
compassion, 21, 57, 58, 59–61, 64
Comprehensive Child Development
Program (CCDP), 98, 99, 100
disappointing results of, 101–102
Comprehensive Employment and
Training Act (CETA), 168
Congressional Digest, 25
Congressional Record, 19, 21
Connecticut, 30, 32, 173
wage-equivalent welfare benefits
in, 76, 77, 78
corporate subsidies
affect relationship of government
and business, 142–43
as alias for corporate welfare,
140–44, 147–48
are beneficial, 146–49
destroy market forces, 144–45
should be abolished, 140–45
Council of Jewish Federations, 68, 69
crack babies, 33, 61–62
Crittenton Homes, 50–51

Daschle, Tom, 34

Democratic Leadership Council, 143,
145
Democrats, 32, 34, 47, 162
District of Columbia, 79, 80, 82
wage-equivalent welfare benefits in,
76, 77, 78
Doherty, Brian, 128
Dole, Bob, 180
Downey, Tom, 124

Economic Policy Institute, 86
Elders, Joycelyn, 155
Engler, John, 43, 44, 178
Estés, Clarissa Pinkola, 17
Europe, 31, 177

Family Support Act (FSA), 1988, 90,
127, 165, 170
Family Support Administration, 129
Farmers Home Administration, 142
fathers. *See* child support.
Ferguson, Sarah, 32
Florida, 36, 55, 128, 144, 188
Folks, Homer, 51
food stamps, 20, 80, 107, 109, 137,
180
food supplements, 20, 71, 81
Forstmann, Theodore J., 144
Fortune 500 firms, 143
Friar, Monica E., 183
Future of Children, The (Aber et al.),
93

Gallaway, Lowell, 37
Gardiner, Karen N., 96
Gephardt, Richard, 31, 32
Gingrich, Newt, 180
government programs
help teen mothers get off welfare,
89–95
con, 96–102
Graduate Equivalency Degree (GED),
95, 98, 101, 102
Graduation, Reality, and Dual Role
Skills (GRADS) program, 91
Granger, Robert, 100
Great Depression, the, 66
Great Society programs, 18, 19, 21,
183
Greenstein, Robert, 86
Gueron, Judith M., 164, 175

Haddam, Jane, 29
Halperin, Samuel, 176, 177
Hartman, David, 75
Hartmann, Heidi, 84, 88
Harvard Business School, 21
Hawaii, 76, 77, 78, 80, 82

Head Start, 32, 33
health care, 84, 87, 97, 191
  in Britain, 30
  costs of, 26
  reform, 27–28
Heckler, Margaret, 124
Heckman, James, 40
Hispanic Americans, 86, 116, 117
homelessness, 43, 44, 60, 169
  and shelters, 61–62, 66
Housing Assistance (Sect. 8), 81, 107,
  108

illegitimate births, 24–25, 50
  increasing rates of, 38, 55, 97
  should be discouraged by welfare
    reform, 54, 153–56
    con, 157–63
  see also single mothers; teen mothers
Illinois, 91, 92, 93 154
immigrants, 18
  are not a burden on welfare system,
    136–39
  should be denied welfare, 132–135
Immigration and Nationality Act, 134
Income Maintenance Experiments,
  39
Industrial Christian Alliance, 63
Insight on the News, 169
Institute for Women's Policy
  Research, 48
Internal Revenue Service (IRS), 125

Jensen, Rita Henley, 114
Job Corps, 176
Job Opportunities and Basic Skills
  (JOBS) Training Program, 90, 91,
  92, 165, 168
  funds necessary to implement, 170,
    171
  has increased number of working
    AFDC recipients, 166
  is prerequisite for time-limited
    welfare, 167
Job Training Partnership Act Title II
  program (JTPA), 175, 176
job training programs, 62–63, 154–56
  are appropriate for welfare
    recipients, 25–26, 87–88, 164–71
    because they promote self-
      sufficiency, 90–94
  are ineffective, 99–102, 172–77
  most promising element of, 176–77
  see also government programs;
    workfare

Kammer, Fred, 65
Kasich, John, 147

Kaslow, Amy, 148
Kemp, Jack, 155
Klein, Joe, 124
Koch, Ed, 168
Kottmeier, Dennis, 127

Lauber, William F., 132
Layzer, Jean, 101
LEARNfare, 36
Learning, Earning, and Parenting
  (LEAP) program, 91, 93, 94
Leonard, Herman B., 183
Levine, Daniel R., 106
Levitan, Sar, 173
Liebmann, George, 49
Los Angeles Times, 19
Lubove, R., 51
Lutheran Social Services, 68, 69

Magaziner, Ira C., 177
Magnet, Myron, 187, 189
Manpower Demonstration Research
  Corporation (MDRC), 97, 100, 154,
  156, 169
  and welfare-related training
    evaluations, 40, 174, 175
Marshall, Ray, 177
Massachusetts, 76, 77, 78, 82, 193
Mathematica Policy Research, 98
Matloff, Norman, 133
Matthews, Merrill, Jr., 60
Maynard, Rebecca A., 93
Mead, Lawrence, 184
Medicaid, 36, 38, 55, 80–81, 109
  costs for immigrants, 133, 139
Medicare, 137, 138
Mexico, 135
Michigan, 43, 143, 179, 180
Mishel, Lawrence, 86
Moore, Kristin, 97
Moore, Stephen, 75, 140
Morra, Linda G., 175
Morton, M.J., 52
Moynihan, Daniel Patrick, 24, 27,
  182
Murray, Charles, 36, 154, 193

Nathan, Richard P., 183
National Conference of Charities and
  Corrections, 51
National Conference of State
  Legislatures (NCSL), 127
National Organization for Women,
  116
National Welfare Rights Union, 162
New Chance program, 94–95, 97–98
  disappointing results of, 100, 101,
    102

New Deal programs, 30, 183
New Jersey, 54, 76, 77, 78, 91
Newsweek, 124
New York, 82, 168, 185
  wage-equivalent welfare benefits,
    76, 77, 78
New York Commission on Relief for
  Widowed Mothers, 51
New York Times, 143, 160, 192
Nilsen, Sigurd, 175, 177
Norton, Rob, 146

Office of Child Support Enforcement
  (OCSE), 127, 129
Offner, Paul, 122
Ohio, 91, 92, 93
Olasky, Marvin, 56

Perkins, Frances, 52, 53
Personal Responsibility Act, 45, 69,
  158, 162
Piven, Frances Fox, 158
Polakow, Valerie, 42
poor people, 16, 45
  are often working people, 70, 76
  are under attack by right-wing
    reformers, 47, 162–63
  and dependency, 28, 38, 52, 58, 84
  lack of compassion for, 57
  need private rehabilitative services,
    55
  stay on welfare
    because of good benefits, 75–82
    because of lack of opportunities,
      83–88
  as stereotyped by welfare debate,
    43, 47–48, 160–61
poverty, 71, 170
  is exacerbated by welfare, 37–39
  and official poverty line, 82, 130
  war on, 36, 58–59
Pregnancy Freedom of Choice Act, 54
Progressive Policy Institute, 147
Project Child, 20

Quayle, Dan, 143

Rachel, Jenifer, 126
racism, 31, 115, 116
Rains, Prudence, 51
Rand Corp., 176
Reader's Digest, 106, 107
Reagan, Ronald, 118, 168
  administration, 33
Reason magazine, 128
Rector, Robert, 37, 132
Red Cross, 61
Reich, Robert, 141, 143, 145, 176, 177

Reilly, G.D., 52
Republicans, 34, 47, 158, 159, 179
Rich, Spencer, 172
Roosevelt, F.D., administration of, 52
Roselius, Rebecca, 40
Rowe, Pat, 89

Salvation Army, 67, 68, 69
San Diego Union-Tribune, 67
schools, 33
  costs, 138
  hot lunch programs, 18
Schroeder, Patricia, 18
Schumpeter, Joseph, 183
Seib, Gerald, 180
Senate Finance Committee, 183, 185
Shalala, Donna, 124
Shapiro, Isaac, 86
Shapiro, Robert J., 147
Shaw, E. Clay, Jr., 188
Sherman, William Tecumseh, 57
Simon, Julian L., 136
single mothers, 39, 82–84, 107–109,
  154, 191
  are large portion of welfare
    recipients, 38
  children of, are at risk, 38–39, 43,
    130
  do not need welfare, 49–55
  and maternity homes, 50, 53–54
  need adequate welfare, 42–48, 88
  see also child care; child support;
    teen mothers
Small Business Administration, 142
Smith, Chris, 54
Smith, Jeffrey, 40
social class differences, 19, 116, 118
Social Contract, 46, 47
Social Security, 33, 60, 80, 137, 138
Spalter-Roth, Roberta, 84, 86, 88
Special Supplemental Food Program
  for Women, Infants, and Children
  (WIC), 81
Stansel, Dean, 140
Stanton, Wayne, 129
stereotypes, 39, 40, 76, 115–16
  "deadbeat dads," 125, 127, 128,
    130, 131, 161
  and media images, 119–20
  "welfare queens," 18, 21, 57, 114,
    158
St. Vincent de Paul Society, 69
Supplemental Security Income/
  Insur-ance (SSI), 66, 134, 135, 137,
  138
Survey of Absent Parents (SOAP), 129
Synthetic Fuels Corporation (SFC),
  142

Tanner, Michael, 35, 75
taxes, 32, 125, 148–49
  breaks vs. subsidies, 145, 148
  Earned Income Tax Credit (EITC),
    27, 33, 87
teen mothers, 24, 25, 38, 109–12,
  160
  disadvantages of, 98–99
  and education, 91, 95, 100–101
  needs of, 90
  should receive assistance from
    families, 53
  and subsequent births, 101–102
  see also charitable aid; government
    programs; single mothers
Teen Parent Demonstration Program,
  90–91, 93, 94, 98
  did not prevent subsequent
    pregnancies, 101
  saw some gains in employment, 100
Texas Supreme Court Commission on
  Child Support and Access, 130
Thatcher, Margaret, 32
Thompson, Tommy G., 179, 186
Tilly, Chris, 83
Twain, Mark, 129
Tyson, Laura, 177

United States, 36, 58, 94, 95, 107
  Census Bureau, 129, 130
  Chinese language publications in,
    133–34
  Commerce Department, 148
  Congress, 130, 131, 141
    gave states flexibility to redesign
      programs, 170
    House of Representatives, 179
      Ways and Means Committee, 134
    is not authorized to subsidize
      business, 144–45
    and origins of AFDC, 158
    Senate Finance Committee, 183,
      185
    and welfare cuts, 68, 82
  Constitution, 68, 144
  Department of Agriculture, 141
    Family Economics Research
      Group, 129
  Department of Education
    Even Start program, 101
  Department of Health and Human
    Services (DHHS), 129
  economic stratification of, 118
  General Accounting Office, 91, 123,
    174
  Labor Department, 175
  needs more apprenticeship
    programs, 177

  takes in elderly of other countries,
    133
United Way, 66, 67, 68
U.S. News & World Report, 119
Utilities Assistance, 81

Vedder, Richard, 37
Village Voice, 32
volunteers, 59, 60, 69

Wall Street Journal, 179
Washington, D.C., 63
Washington Post National Weekly
  Edition, 99, 174
Washington Times, 60, 155, 180
Weber, Vin, 155
welfare, 18, 26
  benefits exceed poverty level in
    every state, 82
  con, 88
  in Europe, 31–32
  is necessity for some women, 84,
    114–121
  is way of life for some women,
    106–13
  is woman's issue, 158–59, 161–62
  pays more than many jobs, 76, 82
  reform, 18
    and block grants, 180, 183
    is necessary, 22–28
    should cut back on level of
      benefits, 77
    should not punish mothers,
      119–21, 157–62
    should promote personal
      responsibility, 186–89
    should require mothers to work,
      131, 156, 171
    should serve needs of poor
      people, 190–93
    threatens reproductive rights of
      women, 119, 159, 162
    see also charitable aid; Clinton,
      Bill, administration; illegitimate
      births
  should be eliminated, 35–41
  should be expanded, 29–34, 87
  should be preserved, 17–21, 84, 88
  should be turned over to the states,
    178–81
    con, 70–71, 182–85
  should require work/job training,
    25, 61, 62–63, 164–71
  time-limits on, 154, 159, 169, 188,
    193
    challenges in implementing,
      166–67
    see also Aid to Families with

Dependent Children
Welfare Reform Act (1988), 70
West Virginia, 154
Wildavsky, Rachel, 106
Wilson, Pete, 180
Wisconsin, 43, 44, 130, 179, 186–89
Women's Employment Network
  (WEN), 26
Women's Policy Research (WPR), 84,
  85
Women with Infant Children (WIC),
  47
Woolsey, Lynn, 190–93
work
  and community service jobs, 154,
    155, 168
  importance of, 26, 28, 63
  often pays less than welfare, 76–77,
    82, 87
  and women, 84–88
Work and Personal Responsibility
  Act, 158, 162
workfare programs, 36, 39, 49, 76, 161
  presume reluctance to work, 159
  Wisconsin model for, 188
Work First, 46–47
Work Incentive Program (WIN), 118,
  120

Youth Policy, 37

Zabin, Laurie, 155